As the pulpit goes, so goes God's people. Wherever preaching is devalued, trivialized, or hijacked by entertainers and charlatans, Christ's sheep are left malnourished and abused. But when God's word is clearly and powerfully proclaimed, supernatural grace is poured out in abundant measure upon willing and believing hearts. In this insightful and practical volume, Paul Shirley traces the indelible line between vibrant preaching and powerful, enduring faith. Bold and convicting exposition may have disappeared from many churches today, but those who've tasted its powerful dynamic always safeguard its preeminence in the body of Christ. If you really want to understand the premium God places on preaching the word as the primary means for spiritual growth, immerse yourself in this book.

Jerry Wragg
President
The Expositors Seminary
Jupiter, FL

One of the main objectives for the biblical expositor is to be conscious of the spiritual growth of his audience as he preaches God's Word. *Expository Sanctification* is an excellent work designed to demonstrate and remind preachers of their role in the sanctification of their people as they proclaim the truths of Scripture. Simple, straight-forward, and thoroughly biblical, Paul Shirley provides practical steps for every expositor for how to emphasize this often neglected element in sermon preparation and delivery.

Steven J. Lawson
President
OnePassion Ministries
Dallas, TX

In this succinct yet profound little book, Dr. Shirley shows the important relationship between expository preaching and progressive sanctification for the life of every believer. Sadly, widespread deficient preaching has met the lack of clear teaching on progressive sanctification, creating a perfect storm. Shirley brings a much-needed corrective to contemporary movements such as the free-grace and gospel sanctification models that have caused so much confusion in contemporary Christianity. He has skillfully displayed the vital relationship of clear, courageous expository preaching to the ongoing work of the Spirit of God in the sanctification of His people. A delightful and very worthwhile read for certain.

Stephen Lonetti
Pastor for Preaching and Vision
Beacon of Hope
St. Paul, MN

For a few years now, I have been hoping to see Paul's work on this subject put into print. He has given much thought to and done much work on the subject of sanctification. His focus on the relationship between preaching and the believer's spiritual growth is greatly needed in the church of our time. I have tremendous respect for Paul as a pastor and a careful and skillful teacher of God's Word. It is with joy that I recommend this book, and I hope all our people will read it.

Richard Caldwell
Pastor-Teacher
Founders Baptist Church
Spring, TX

Too many Christians listen to too many sermons with too little thoughtfulness. And too many of the same struggle to gain traction in their spiritual growth. Paul Shirley shows that there is a connection here. When it comes to listening to sermons, there is a correlation between hearing and holiness, between listening and living, and between preaching and perspective. This a book on preaching, but it is not written for preachers. It's a book designed for anyone who desires to leverage the power of God's preached Word for the good and growth of their own souls.

Rick Holland
Sr. Pastor
Mission Road Bible Church
Kansas City

It certainly seems strange to say it, but the obvious point of preaching is to see your hearers become progressively conformed to the image of the Lord Jesus Christ. With what Holy Scripture itself instructs us as preachers, who could possibly argue the point? Yet it seems that in our own day, many of those who regularly occupy pulpits don't always appear to be doing so expositorily, and with the progressive sanctification of the listener as their chief end. This is precisely why Paul Shirley has written this book you hold in your hands. So as to press the point home once again—and he does so quite admirably—Shirley reminds us that the very essence of a preacher's expository ministry is to see the flock of God spiritually conformed to the Son of God, both individually and corporately. He defines both the principles of biblical exposition and sanctification, and then shows us how the two come together as God Himself intends. If you are an expositor and are committed to seeing your people become more like Jesus, then reading this fine volume will more than reward your effort.

Dr. Lance Quinn
Senior Pastor
Bethany Church on the Hill
Thousand Oaks, CA

Paul Shirley has written a masterful book on the role of expository preaching in the spiritual growth of Christians. If you want to read a book that will help you learn how to listen to your pastor's sermons and grow from them, then this is the book for you. I highly recommend it.

Dr. Steven Kreloff
Pastor-Teacher
Lakeside Community Chapel
Clearwater, FL

Expository
Sanctification

Paul Shirley

KRESS
BIBLICAL
RESOURCES

ISBN: 978-1-934952-48-1

DEDICATION

To my beloved wife, Elyse, without whom this book never would have been completed. I see your patience, love, and encouragement in every word of this project. I've been blessed to marry for sanctification.

ACKNOWLEDGMENTS

The foundations for this book began when I was a kid and my dad modeled the truth and got our family to churches that taught God's word. Additionally, the idea that preaching is powerful for spiritual growth immediately made sense to me because I have benefited from the faithful preaching of so many men over the years. My formal training at The Expositors Seminary and The Master's Seminary cemented the importance of preaching for holiness in my mind.

I am deeply grateful for my ongoing and edifying friendship with Richard Caldwell, who read every single draft of this book. I listen to his sermons on my phone every Monday, and I am always edified by the clarity he provides when he preaches God's word. Richard is an eminently gifted preacher, whose gospel proclamation has reached thousands of souls.

I am also indebted to Jerry Wragg. I don't know anyone who understands the nuanced workings of the inner man more clearly than Jerry, which is evident in his preaching. When I listen to him preach, I marvel at his gift for bringing out the heart implications of a text for his congregation. Jerry is a modern-day Puritan whose leadership has had a massive impact on so many men.

The men who most supported the writing of this book are the elders I have served alongside at Grace Community Church in Delaware. Roy Wilson, who is now with the Lord, was the most mature Christian man I've ever met and loved preaching more than anyone I've ever known. Jim O'Neill has been the source of constant support and encouragement for me since my very first sermon at our church. Jared Cooper's love for preaching and explosive growth under the ministry of the word is part of what led to this study; he is a Proverbs 18:24 friend to me. These men are a joy to serve alongside, and so is the congregation we serve. Our church loves to hear the truth, and they love anyone who will faithfully teach them the truth.

In addition to my church, my family makes life and ministry such a joy. My three girls, Rebecca, Makaylah, and Sarah, joyfully sit through their daddy's sermons and endure his questions at Sunday lunch. Our family discipleship times after dinner each night are my favorite teaching opportunities because in those times, I see the power of God's word working on the hearts of those whom I love the most. I pray for each of my girls that faith will come by hearing (Rom 10:17).

My wife, Elyse, is my help-mate in life and ministry. Her presence makes my load lighter, and her encouragement makes my burdens more bearable. Everything I do is sweeter when she is involved. I treasure her input on everything, which is why I had her read every word of this book before it was published. She sacrifices much to free me up to study, shepherd, and write.

CONTENTS

1
THE NEED FOR EXPOSITORY SANCTIFICATION

Why do we have to sit through so many sermons? As a Christian, has this thought ever occurred to you? Week after week, we go to church and sit under the preaching of God's word. In some ways it is so normal that it has become expected, but have you ever thought about the role preaching plays in your spiritual life? In the normal course of an average Christian life a believer will most likely listen to thousands of sermons, but not many of us have given much thought to why that is and how God designed the sermon to feed our souls. Many believers, as well as pastors, continue to follow the pattern of weekly preaching but know very little of the power of preaching in their lives.

The place of the pulpit in progressive sanctification is a subject that deserves our attention because, by God's design, preaching is the most powerful resource for spiritual growth in the church's arsenal. In other words, biblical preaching is the primary means of grace for sanctification. No personal discipline, new strategy, or life-changing experience can rival the power of preaching for sanctification. In practice, this means that if you want to grow in your Christian life, you need to find and devour spiritually deep and biblically thorough preaching. Think about it—how many mature Christians do you know who have not been heavily influenced by faithful preaching? If you are anything like me, the answer is none. There is an inextricable link between strong preaching and spiritual maturity, which means if you want to grow in the Lord, you need to submit to faithful preaching as a source of sanctifying grace.

Preaching and sanctification are bound to one another in God's plan, which means they must be found together in the local church. A church faithfully

1

proclaiming the word of God will produce Christians faithfully growing closer to God. However, sermons that distort God's truth will distract believers from this primary means of grace and alienate them from the practical help God has promised for their lives. In other words, weak pulpits and weak Christians go hand-in-hand; a church failing to proclaim the word of God produces Christians failing to grow closer to God.

Together, preaching and sanctification are two of the church's preeminent responsibilities, which is why God commands the church to preach His word (2 Tim 4:2) and to be holy as He is holy (1 Pt 1:15). The power to fulfill both of these responsibilities comes from God, but that does not negate the fact that they are responsibilities. This fact seems to be lost on many preachers as well as congregants. The twin responsibilities of preaching and sanctification are too often misunderstood, ignored, and in some cases even opposed.

THREATS TO SANCTIFICATION

Consider the church's responsibility with regard to sanctification. The New Testament (NT) prioritizes the holiness of God's people. Its pages are teeming with practical exhortations to personal holiness as well as theological explanations of this key doctrine. In their writings, the apostles made sanctification a substantive part of the foundation of the church. However, the church has not always built on this corner of the foundation, especially in recent days. J. I. Packer observed that "in the past, the uncompromising evangelical quest for holiness was awesome in its intensity. Yet that which was formerly a priority and a passion has become a secondary matter for us who bear the evangelical name today."[1] What has happened to derail our focus on sanctification? The greatest external assaults on holiness have come from lethargy, licentiousness, legalism, and libertinism.

Lethargy

Lethargy is the silent assassin of sanctification. The cares of this world and the exertion of spiritual discipline tend to dampen the church's enthusiasm for sanctification. In many churches, personal growth is the exception rather than the rule. All the while, no one seems to notice the problem. A low view of conversion contributes to the situation, but a lethargic view of

---

[1] J. I. Packer, *Keep in Step with the Spirit: Finding Fullness in Our Walk with God* (Grand Rapids: Baker Books, 2005), 83.

sanctification must also be considered as a cause of the worldliness we find in the church. Apathy toward the things of the Lord is a slow-release poison to spiritual growth. The Laodicean problem has become an epidemic in the contemporary church; when it comes to sanctification, we are nauseatingly lukewarm.

Licentiousness

Licentiousness is the perennial rival of sanctification. It does the most damage on a visceral level by appealing to our base emotions and tempting our natural desires. We are so excited by our love for things of this world that we possess little passion for holiness. The lust of the flesh and the prospect of instant gratification make incremental growth in godliness seem passé. To many, the ethics of biblical sanctification feel more like the cultural moorings of a previous generation than the commands of a holy God. Increasingly, sanctification does not "feel right" to the modern man, but licentiousness feels so good. When our base emotions are calling the shots like this, we are certain to have a Corinthian problem of sanctification in the church—we will be worldly.

Legalism

Legalism is the default opponent of sanctification. No matter how many times it raises its ugly head, the temptation to rely on human effort to produce spiritual results will always be alluring. What makes a system of works so seductive? For starters, the sheer productivity of legalism makes it practically appealing. Pragmatism always sells better than godliness. Why worry about the tediously humble and, at times, imperceptible process of heart change, when an easily white-washed tomb seems to get the job done? Additionally, growth by bare human effort feeds our pride. Legalism appeals to us because we are appealing to ourselves. Rules, regulations, and requirements seem attainable by human power, whereas, love and faith require the divine assistance of grace. We would rather do it ourselves, or die trying. The inherent and incessant bravado of legalism eschews the sanctifying grace God has promised us. That is to say, legalism makes sanctification impossible because God opposes the proud and gives grace to the humble. Every attempt to squeeze holiness from faithless effort is just the Galatian problem revived; it is the distortion of gospel truth.

Libertinism

Libertinism seems like the safest opponent of sanctification. In reality it is the most deceptive, pervasive, and possibly the most dangerous influence in the church today. This opponent dissolves the law of God in the name of the gospel. It has been known by different names throughout church history, but the most extreme form has rightly been called antinomianism, which literally means "against the law." At the heart of libertinism is the idea that you can be a Christian and be free from the authority of Christ. R.C. Sproul was convinced that "this heresy is rampant. In fact, we are living in a period of pervasive antinomianism in the church."[2] Since it is so common, it deserves a little extra attention.

The Bible would call a system like this "lawlessness" but the Devil conceals this antagonist in more alluring terminology. Modern iterations of this opponent have even crept into our thinking by re-packaging it under the labels of "free grace" and "gospel-centered" sanctification. With marketing like this, it is easy to see why libertinism seems like the safest opponent of sanctification. As Kevin DeYoung explains, it even seems to appeal to our theological sensibilities:

> Among conservative Christians there is sometimes the mistaken notion that if we are truly gospel-centered we won't talk about rules or imperatives or moral exertion. We are so eager not to confuse indicatives (what God has done) and imperatives (what we should do) that we get leery of letting biblical commands lead uncomfortably to convictions of sin. We're scared of words like diligence, effort, and duty. Pastors don't know how to preach the good news in their sermons and still strongly exhort churchgoers to cleanse themselves from every defilement of body and spirit (2 Cor. 7:1). We know legalism (salvation by law keeping) and antinomianism (salvation without the need for law keeping) are both wrong, but antinomianism feels like a much safer danger.[3]

Much of the confusion over this issue can be attributed to the theological climate of the church today. In many quarters of the church, a Reformed view of justification has been re-discovered. The imputation of Christ's righteousness as the legal ground for the believer's standing before God has moved to the front page of contemporary theology, which is great news. However, many believers never seem to make it past the headlines about justification above the fold on page one to read the rest of the story. They fail to do what the reformers did, continue reforming. As a result, the

---

[2] R. C. Sproul, *Everyone's a Theologian: An Introduction to Systematic Theology,* (Sanford, FL: Reformation Trust Publishing, 2014) 251.

[3] Kevin DeYoung, *The Hole in Our Holiness: Filling the Gap between Gospel Passion and the Pursuit of Godliness* (Wheaton, IL: Crossway Books, 2012), 19.

biblical view of sanctification has been neglected in favor of trite gospel-sounding platitudes. For instance, one shooting star in the "free grace" movement once famously defined progressive sanctification as "the daily hard work of going back to the reality of our justification."[4] In this view of sanctification, and those like it, the multifaceted doctrine of sanctification has been essentially reduced to one word, contemplation. If a Christian will simply think about his justification, he will somehow feel like obeying and automatically get victory over sin. Inevitably, when this kind of passivity does not lead to victory over sin, proponents of sanctification by contemplation will simply claim that personally holiness doesn't matter all that much anyway since we have already been justified. Strangely, some teachers adamantly maintain this paradigm is the only one able to produce true spiritual growth and then tell you not to worry when it doesn't work.

The libertine view of growth in holiness is nothing more than "let go and let God" with a nuanced justification tacked onto it; a strange modern-day mixture of Calvinism and quietism. In many ways, it is similar to the non-lordship view of salvation, which John MacArthur described as "a deficient doctrine of salvation. It is justification without sanctification...."[5]

There is something seductive about this view of sanctification. It magnifies the gloriously true doctrine of justification and at the same time gets us off the hook from doing the hard work of sanctification. Theologically, it is as close as you can get to having your cake and eating it too. There is just one little problem: this is not how the Bible speaks of our sanctification. The Bible uses verbs like strive, work, battle, and kill to speak of our role in sanctification. Grace-empowered submission is the key, not the bare contemplation of grace. You are not being too hard on yourself when you hate sin and strive for victory over it in your life. Libertinism may seem like the safest enemy, but it cannot produce what it promises or what we need.

Lingering Sin

These ideological opponents are not the only threats in the battle for sanctification. The lingering sin in our own hearts is even more dangerous, and adds an additional layer of difficulty to the external challenges of sanctification. Remaining sin—the ongoing influence of sinful patterns, thoughts, and desires—is a constant reality in the life of every believer. Our own flesh rages within us, tempting us to make a return visit to the enemy

---

[4] Tullian Tchividjian, *Jesus + Nothing = Everything* (Wheaton, IL: Crossway Books, 2011), 95.
[5] John MacArthur, Jr., *The Gospel According to Jesus: What is Authentic Faith?*, *Rev. and expanded anniversary ed.*, (Grand Rapids: Zondervan Publishing, 2008), 38.

camp which used to be our home base. Every ideological threat to sanctification was conceived in the dark recesses of man's natural heart and every opponent to sanctification—lethargy, licentiousness, legalism, and libertinism—has a corner of the heart in which to hide. This means that progress in sanctification will require protection from the opponents all around us and purification from sinfulness dwelling within us.

THE NEED FOR SANCTIFICATION

What the church needs is a defense from the external threats and an offense for the internal threats. We need a fortress to protect us from Satan's schemes and a scalpel to remove our own remaining sin. What could possibly possess such power and precision? What resource can we call on to destroy sin and heal our hearts at the same time? What instrument simultaneously cuts and mends?

God has given us the grace we need for holiness, and we find this grace in the Scriptures. The living and active word of God is the only instrument capable of meeting this need. The only way to avoid the various distortions of holiness is to look to the grace found in God's word. Only when we confront the roadblocks to holiness with the truth of God will we find the help we need to be more like Jesus.

Second Corinthians 10:3-5 invites us to look to Scripture as a "bunker busting" weapon against rebel thoughts:

> For though we walk in the flesh, we are not waging war according to the flesh. For the weapons of our warfare are not of the flesh but have divine power to destroy strongholds. We destroy arguments and every lofty opinion raised against the knowledge of God, and take every thought captive to obey Christ ….

Additionally, Hebrews 4:12 describes the precision of the word to mount an offensive against the pockets of resistance in our own hearts, "For the word of God is living and active, sharper than any two-edged sword, piercing to the division of soul and of spirit, of joints and of marrow, and discerning the thoughts and intentions of the heart." God's word is powerful enough to defend against an invasion of error, and precise enough to purge an insurgency of sin.

A preaching need

Because the hindrances to sanctification are so subtly deceptive, we not only need the word of God in our lives, we need it preached to us. We need the definitiveness of the preached word to pin us into submission under the authority of Scripture; the clarity of expository sermons to help us understand the nuance of divine truth in our lives; and the influence of public shepherding to exhort us to live in accordance with what God's word declares. The church needs preaching that will unleash the sanctifying power of the Bible in our lives. This is the kind of preaching that can kill the enemy insurgents within the camp and defend us from the enemy incursion from outside the camp. We need preaching that will powerfully wield the two-edged sword to destroy the enemy encampments.

But here, as we consider preaching, we run into another problem. A quick survey of the landscape reveals a disheartening lack of preaching for sanctification. The sobering assessment of Walter Kaiser is that "the famine of the Word continues in massive proportion in most places in North America."[6] As a number of hungry believers could confirm, many pulpits simply are not preaching for sanctification. Pulpiteers cater to the opponents of sanctification rather than confront them. Lethargic preachers stand before lethargic people without desperate calls to mortify sin—his only urgency is to get to lunch in time. Worse, licentious pastors set a standard of immorality in the church from the top down. Their preaching and example encourage immaturity and immorality; their own stunted growth and stagnant preaching demotes sin to a common misstep rather than an offense to God. On the other end of the spectrum, legalistic pastors scold people for not adhering to the preferences and rules they personally use to define holiness. And when you grow weary of that you can find the libertine pastor down the street who warns only of becoming like the legalist pastor you used to sit under. Caught up in all of this, otherwise good preachers are becoming either trigger happy or gun shy with the Scriptures. They find themselves confused amidst the competing ideas, torn between extremes, and struggling with what to avoid and who to attack.

A pressing need

All things considered, two of the church's most important responsibilities–preaching and sanctification–have fallen on hard times. This is no coincidence. There is a connection between the poor preaching we see in so many corners of evangelicalism and the stagnant pursuits of holiness

---

[6] Walter C. Kaiser Jr., *Revive Us Again* (Nashville: Broadman & Holman, 1999), 166.

experienced by so many evangelical Christians. Sure, there are multiple factors that contribute to the process of sanctification, but a congregation simply cannot grow beyond the maturity of the preaching they sit under. God designed the preaching of His word to mature His people, and when His word is not faithfully proclaimed from the pulpit there will not be consistent growth in the pew. Poor preaching stunts growth in sanctification. We see this reality playing on a loop throughout church history because we keep hitting the repeat button.

Clearly, there is a great deal of confusion in the Church on the doctrine of sanctification, and even more confusion about what kind of preaching will equip Christians in the process of sanctification. Christians struggle to understand what they should expect in their own sanctification, they do not know exactly what they should expect from the pulpit, and they are largely untaught on the importance of preaching in their spiritual growth. Most Christians want to grow in their in their walk with the Lord, but few recognize how the sermons they listen to will affect their growth. This is why the church needs to recalibrate its view on sanctification and the role of preaching in this work of grace. The Lord designed preaching to have a sanctifying effect, but, in order to benefit from this means of grace, God's people must understand the how sanctification works and how preaching fits into this process.

The goal of this book is to provide the church with a practical model for utilizing preaching as a means of grace for sanctification. In other words, I want you to see how biblical preaching can help you grow in personal holiness. The average Christian will listen to thousands of sermons over the course of his Christian life, and the prayer for this work is that it will equip believers to benefit from the preaching they hear. This is not a technical work on preaching for pastors; it is a practical paradigm for how God designed preaching to benefit all of His people. This study will help you understand what you should expect from preaching and how preaching can benefit your spiritual growth. Expositors of God's word certainly need to grasp its power to change people, but laymen also need to understand the priority of preaching in their own spiritual growth. *Powerful preaching produces personal holiness.*

2
THE HOLY REQUIREMENT OF SANCTIFICATION

There are many good reasons to study the subject of holiness. For starters, God is holy, and it is good to think about God. Additionally, the Bible says no one can see God apart from holiness (Heb 12:14)—so that's important. To that we could add that there are a lot of benefits to practical holiness such as being a better spouse, a more faithful parent, possessing personal peace, and so on. These are all good reasons to examine the biblical concept of holiness, but the most important reason for us to study holiness may be the fact that God has saved us to be holy. Holiness is not an optional addendum to gospel grace, it is at the heart of God's redemptive work. God saves us from our sins and declares us righteous so that He can make us holy. From election (Eph 1:4) to glorification (Eph 5:27), God's sanctifying purpose is the holiness of His people.

Sanctification, by definition, requires holiness. The word "sanctified" in both its Latin and Greek roots means "to be made holy." Thus, in order to properly understand the reality of sanctification in our lives, we must first understand the concept of holiness. But, let's be honest, personal holiness is not the most popular topic in the church today. Our own carnal tendencies combined with a lot of poor teaching make this a topic we don't naturally gravitate toward. When confronted with the agonizing task of detaching ourselves from the remaining vestiges of sin in our hearts, it is so much easier to avoid the topic altogether. Sadly, the tendency in our hearts to neglect the pursuit of holiness seems to be rarely confronted with biblical truth. In fact, it is just the opposite. Deficient views of holiness are being disseminated to the church with alarming frequency. You've likely heard holiness teaching that was merely a preacher using his conscience to lord over his people. You've likely also heard recent teaching that claims an overemphasis on holiness only leads to despair. God's people are being taught to think wrongly about the role of holiness in their lives. One extreme distorts holiness through legalism and the other ignores it altogether with libertinism.

Many Christians, having heard so little of holiness from the pulpit, give little or no thought to its place in their spiritual life. As a result, their view of holiness is so anemic that they confuse holiness with legalism. Some even find ways to resent appeals for holiness in the name of grace. On the other end of the spectrum, some perpetually emphasize personal holiness, at least their own conception of it. Their holiness is attainable through rules, because they think of it in strictly moral terms, as if outward behavior was the only characteristic of holiness. Thus, one side ignores holiness and the other distorts it. Thankfully, the Bible presents a thorough and nuanced view that rises above the morass of deficient views of holiness.

A BIBLICAL EXAMINATION OF HOLINESS

We are first introduced to the concept of holiness in the Old Testament (OT), where to be holy is to be set apart and distinguished from that which is common. It is a purity and consistency that excludes any amalgamation, dilution, or compromise. Yes, there is an ethical component to holiness that requires obedience, but there is so much more to it than that. In fact, when the Bible uses holiness language, it does so in three distinct ways: intrinsic holiness, consecrated holiness, and reflective holiness. To put it another way, the OT uses the word holy to describe that which is essential to God's nature, that which is specially consecrated to God's service, and that which is ethically reflective of God's character.

Intrinsic holiness

To say that something is intrinsic means that it naturally belongs, which is the case with holiness and the character of God. He is holy, and all holiness flows from the intrinsic holiness which is found only in His divine character. Everything He is and all that He does is distinguished by the perfect holiness which permeates every one of His attributes and acts. As R.C. Sproul reminds us, transcendent separation characterizes the holiness found in God:

> When the Bible calls God holy, it means primarily that God is transcendentally separate. He is so far above and beyond us that He seems almost totally foreign to us. To be holy is to be "other," to be different in a special way.[7]

His being and His behavior transcend creation, and His utter perfection separates Him from the defilement of imperfection. He is incomprehensibly distinguished in everything that He does and everything that He is. In the words of the prophet, "There is none like you, O Lord; you are great, and your name is great in might" (Jer 10:6).

God's transcendent otherness is the most obvious manifestation of His holy nature. Since it is an eternal attribute, however, the reality of divine holiness must penetrate even deeper than the language of separation is able to communicate. God was holy before there was anything from which to be separate. He isn't holy because He is separate, He is separate because He is holy. God's holiness is the essential purity of His perfections and the immutable consistency of His nature. Or, to paraphrase what YHWH said to Moses, "I am who I am, which makes this holy ground." (Exod 3:14).

God's holiness is the foundational principle of theology proper and the preeminent feature of OT revelation. Isaiah 6:3 encapsulates the message of the OT, "Holy, holy, holy is the Lord of hosts; the whole earth is filled with his glory." The angels in Isaiah 6 antiphonally magnified the unapproachable, unimaginable, and unrelenting intrinsic holiness of God which is first revealed in the OT.

The NT articulates the same concepts of holiness found in the OT, however, it does so with major developments. For instance, the intrinsic holiness of God is indelibly engraved on the pages of the NT just as in the OT. However, in the NT the concept of intrinsic holiness becomes explicitly trinitarian. The NT explicitly reveals the "holy, holy, holy" God of Isaiah 6:3 as the Triune God—Father, Son, and Holy Spirit. Each member of the Godhead equally possesses the searing purity of perfect holiness. The Father is described as holy (Jn 15:11), the Son is described as holy (1 Pt 3:15), and the Spirit is described as holy (Mk 1:8; 3:29; Acts 1:2; 4:8; 5:32; Rom 15:13). Thus, the NT fully develops the concept of intrinsic holiness by presenting the Triune God as the touchstone for all holiness. All of this means that from a biblical perspective, when we speak of holiness, we are

---

[7] R. C. Sproul, *The Holiness of God, Revised and Expanded* (Wheaton, IL: Tyndale House Publishers, 1998), 38.

first and foremost speaking of the Lord, Who is "majestic in holiness, [and] awesome in glorious deeds" (Exod 15:11).

Consecrated holiness

Consecrated holiness describes objects and individuals that have been specifically dedicated to the service of God. For instance, in the OT many of the objects used in the temple worship were described as holy despite the fact that they were inanimate objects. One example of this concept of holiness is the altar on which sacrifices were to be made:

> Thus you shall do to Aaron and to his sons, according to all that I have commanded you. Through seven days shall you ordain them, and every day you shall offer a bull as a sin offering for atonement. Also you shall purify the altar, when you make atonement for it, and shall anoint it to consecrate it. Seven days you shall make atonement for the altar and consecrate it, and the altar shall be most holy. Whatever touches the altar shall become holy. (Exod 29:35–37).

Clearly, this altar was not holy in the sense that it was obedient to the law and godly in character—it was a lifeless object. It was holy because it had been set apart by God for the purpose of worship.

Another example of consecrated holiness is found in the furniture used in the tabernacle:

> With it you shall anoint the tent of meeting and the ark of the testimony, and the table and all its utensils, and the lampstand and its utensils, and the altar of incense, and the altar of burnt offering with all its utensils and the basin and its stand. You shall consecrate them, that they may be most holy. Whatever touches them will become holy (Exod 30:26–29).

The clear meaning of holiness in these contexts is something that has been set apart by God for the purpose of worship. Thus, consecrated holiness is a position established by God for the purpose of worship which depends on the decree and designation of God.

This category of holiness is not limited to the OT. The NT picks up on the concept of consecrated holiness and sheds fresh gospel light on it. Previously, items such as furniture, sacrifices, days, festivals, and locations were among the many objects set apart as holy for a specific purpose. Not only were these items consecrated for service, they were necessary for worship. That all changed, however, with the dawning of the Church in the NT.

Now, God's people worship the Father in spirit and truth, not in holy places (Jn 4:19-24). We do not need to observe holy "days and months and seasons and years" (Gal 4:10). Nor do we need to ritually purify ourselves and our sacrifices for worship (Col 2:10-17; Heb 10:1-10). We do not need objects that have been consecrated for worship, because we are the objects that have been consecrated for worship. Under the New Covenant, God's people have been set apart as a living sacrifice, holy and acceptable to God for spiritual worship:

> I appeal to you therefore, brothers, by the mercies of God, to present your bodies as a living sacrifice, holy and acceptable to God, which is your spiritual worship. Do not be conformed to this world, but be transformed by the renewal of your mind, that by testing you may discern what is the will of God, what is good and acceptable and perfect. (Rom 12:1-2)

The NT teaches that every Christian now possesses a consecrated holiness before God. God made us holy (i.e. "saints") so that we can serve Him in every aspect of our lives. We have been consecrated by God (positional sanctification) so that we can personally worship Him (progressive sanctification). Just as the elements of worship under the Mosaic covenant were ceremonially washed so that they could serve in worship of God's people, we are redemptively cleansed through the work of Christ so that we can serve the Lord through a life of worship.

Reflective holiness

Reflective holiness describes the morally upright behavior of God's people, who reflect God's holiness by living according to His righteous standards. This concept of holiness does not appear in the OT as frequently as the first two, but it is, nonetheless, required. In fact, we find the foundations for reflective holiness in the first chapters of Genesis, where man was created to bear the image of God. Much could be said about what it means to bear the image of God, but at the very least it includes reflecting His holy nature. We were created to be holy as God is holy, which is why we find so many commands to this end in the Scripture. God's holiness demands the holiness of His people. For instance, Deuteronomy 28:9 says, "The Lord will establish you as a people holy to himself, as he has sworn to you, if you keep the commandments of the Lord your God and walk in his ways."

Then, the rest of Deuteronomy 28 describes the blessings promised for reflecting God's holiness and the curses threatened for failing to do so. Put simply, reflective holiness requires obedience on the part of God's people.

The NT expands on the importance of ethical expressions of holiness by placing significant emphasis on holiness at a heart level (1 Cor. 7:34; 1 Pet. 1:16). With a new perspective, a substantiated promise, and an endowment of spiritual power, the NT applies the implications of reflective holiness to the inner man. When Jesus exposited the demands of reflective holiness from the OT, he made it clear that true holiness requires pure motives:

> You have heard that it was said, 'You shall not commit adultery.' But I say to you that everyone who looks at a woman with lustful intent has already committed adultery with her in his heart. If your right eye causes you to sin, tear it out and throw it away. For it is better that you lose one of your members than that your whole body be thrown into hell. And if your right hand causes you to sin, cut it off and throw it away. For it is better that you lose one of your members than that your whole body go into hell. (Mt 5:27-30)

Members of the New Covenant have God's law written on their hearts (Jer 31:33) so that they can reflect God's holiness with their lives. As Spirit-born, blood-bought, children of God, we are finally able to do what we were created to do—bear the image of the holy God. Believers, who have been separated unto God through the Gospel, are required to live an increasingly righteous life to reflect that separation.

Collectively, the Bible presents holiness as a transcendent otherness found in the immutably pure character of the Triune God, a dedicated service in the worship of the worthy God, and a reflective purity in obedience to the authoritative God. To put it another way, holiness is a reality epitomized by God, a position determined by God, and requirement demanded by God. These concepts of holiness form the foundation for a biblical theology of holiness.

THE PERFECT EMBODIMENT OF HOLINESS

A study of holiness would not be complete without an examination of the holiness of Christ. A true understanding of holiness cannot be had apart from a true appreciation of Christ. When Christ became a man—taking on a human nature—he also became the perfect embodiment of holiness. The holiness revealed in the scripture is "fleshed out" by Christ, who fulfills each concept, meets every requirement, and manifest the full glory of true holiness.

The Holy One

With respect to intrinsic holiness, Christ is the Holy One who manifests the nature of God. Hebrews 1:3 calls Him "the radiance of the glory of God and the exact imprint of his nature...." His miraculous works on earth proved to demons and disciples alike that He is "the holy one of God" (Mk 1:24; Lk 4:34; Jn 6:69). This was not just the assessment of those around Him; in Revelation 3:7, Christ describes Himself as "the holy one." The Gospels confirm that everything true about the intrinsic holiness of God is true of Christ.

The Consecrated One

Christ is also the Consecrated One, who was set apart by God for the purpose of accomplishing salvation, which is why Jesus described Himself as the One "whom the Father consecrated and sent into the world" (Jn 10:36). Just as the Father ordained and consecrated the sacrifices of the OT, Jesus was consecrated as a holy sacrifice unto God. By divine decree, Jesus was designated as the acceptable substitute for sinners and "set apart" by the Father as the Holy Savior. It was not just the Father who set Christ apart—the entire Trinity participated in this consecrating work: Jesus consecrated Himself (Jn 17:19), and He was anointed by the Spirit (Lk 4:18) for this purpose. All this to say, the concept of consecrated holiness finds fulfillment in Christ.

The Righteous One

Finally, Christ is the Righteous One who perfectly reflected God's holiness with His righteous life. The first Adam was made in the image of God to reflect the holiness of God, but he failed. Through his sin, Adam fell short of the glory of God and violated God's holiness. Where the first Adam failed, the Second Adam did not. The Second Adam's life is inerrantly described as "holy, innocent, unstained, [and] separated from sinners" (Heb 7:26). He is the only human being of whom it can be said that "he committed no sin, neither was deceit found in his mouth" (1 Pt 1:22). As a man, Jesus perfectly reflected the holiness of God. His earthly existence was an exposition of heaven's holiness. When Christ took on flesh and dwelt among us, He became the perfect human reflection of God's holiness, and the standard-bearer of reflective holiness.

THE REQUIREMENT OF HOLINESS

The biblical concept of holiness established by the OT, developed in the NT, and fulfilled in Christ, defines what it means to be holy. These concepts govern how God's people are to think about holiness, and the more our minds contemplate these biblical concepts, the more we are confronted with the holy requirement of sanctification. Each biblical expression of holiness creates a burden for us in sanctification. Intrinsic holiness requires us to look to God's holiness as the criterion for our sanctification, because we must be holy as God is holy (Lev 11:44-45; 1 Pt 1:15-16.) and perfect as our Heavenly Father is perfect (Mt 5:48). Consecrated holiness requires the work of God in our sanctification to set us apart for His service, because only those items that have been divinely chosen by God can be considered holy—holiness is not merely a matter of personal choice. Reflective holiness requires our effort in sanctification to ethically display God's character, because no one can have assurance that they will see God apart from some evidence of an ethical expression of holiness (Heb 12:14).

Sanctification demands holiness at all levels from the believer, but how could we possibly meet this holy requirement? How can we bear the burden of holiness in the work of sanctification? The answer is that we cannot. We do not possess the perfection or the power needed for holiness. We are not God, cannot set ourselves apart to God, and would not live righteously for God. In ourselves and by ourselves, sanctification is impossible. So where can we look for our sanctification?

First Corinthians 1:30 compels us to look to the only possible source of holiness for sinners: Christ. He is the one "who became to us wisdom from God, righteousness and sanctification and redemption." Our Savior became sanctification for us so that through His incarnation, the gap between God's intrinsic holiness and our deficient sinfulness could be bridged. He was consecrated for our consecration, and His holy life empowers our holy living. "We have been sanctified through the offering of the body of Jesus Christ, once for all" (Heb 10:10). Thus, our only hope of holiness is to "hide our unholiness in the wounds of Christ as Moses hid himself in the cleft of the rock while the glory of God passed by."[8] All of this means that in order to conform to holy the requirement of sanctification, we must entrust ourselves to Christ.

---

[8] A.W. Tozer, *The Knowledge of the Holy* (New York: Harper & Row, 1961), 107.

By faith, we are brought into union with Christ in order to be conf[...]
God's standard of holiness. Through our faith-union with Christ, the[...]
intrinsic holiness of God is pleased with us, and through that same unio[...]
we are set apart to please God with our reflective holiness. Jesus is not on[...]
the standard of holiness; he is the source of our holiness. Because Jesus
possesses intrinsic holiness, consecrated holiness, and reflective holiness,
He is able to endow us with the holy requirements of sanctification. We
must be "in Christ" to be sanctified.

In Christ, we are reckoned holy because of His holiness. In Christ, the holy
requirement of sanctification has been met and is being realized in us. In
Christ, we are indwelt by His Spirit to empower us to live holy lives. In
Christ, we possess the perfect sinlessness, the purifying sacrifice, and the
practical support we need for sanctification. In Christ, we have holiness, we
are holy, and we can be holy.

It is no exaggeration when Joel Beeke asserts that "the primary secret of
sanctification is a personal and vital union with Jesus Christ."[9] Union with
Christ is the relationship between a believer and Christ from which all the
benefits of salvation are derived. In the words of the apostle Paul, God "has
blessed us in Christ with every spiritual blessing in the heavenly places"
(Eph 1:3). Every spiritual blessing—including holiness—springs forth out
of our union with Christ. In Christ, we are set apart as holy, and we are
empowered to pursue holiness.

The OT introduces us to holiness, the NT develops our understanding of
holiness, Christ fulfills all holiness, and in Christ, holiness operates in the
spiritual growth of the believer.

---

[9] Joel Beeke, "Introduction to The Gospel Mystery of Sanctification" in Walter Marshall, *The Gospel Mystery of Sanctification* (Grand Rapids: Reformation Heritage Books, 2013), v.

3
THE BIBLICAL TRAJECTORY OF SANCTIFICATION

On April 11, 1970, at 2:11 p.m., the Apollo 13 spacecraft launched into orbit seeking to perform the third lunar landing in history before safely returning to earth. However, an explosion in oxygen tank two irrevocably scrubbed the original mission. Three American astronauts were stranded in space and running out of consumables. Their only hope of survival was something called a free-return trajectory. Using strategic burns of the engine on the lunar landing module, they would have to maneuver the ship into the perfect trajectory to slingshot themselves around the moon and back to earth. By God's grace, they succeeded. The precision required for success is lost on those of us who don't work for NASA, but if the ship did not stay on the perfect trajectory, they would have lost the needed gravitational pull from the moon and skipped off into deep space. One degree of deviation in any direction would have been the difference between life and death.

In many ways, our understanding of sanctification is similar to a free-return trajectory. There are few doctrines that require the precision and nuance this doctrine calls for. Historical theology is replete with examples of deviations that lead to heresy, and neglect that leads to apostasy. Legalism rears its head when a skewed view of progressive sanctification becomes the centerpiece of theology. Antinomianism finds its roots in a truncated view of positional sanctification. And perfectionism–the idea that some Christians reach a state of perfection in this life–contorts the eschatological goal of sanctification into a present reality. As these common historical errors demonstrate, deviation in any direction will lead us drastically off course, turning a free-return trajectory into a free-falling disaster. This is why we must be guided by Scripture, which provides three references points to keep us on a safe trajectory in sanctification.

THE POSITIONAL REALITY OF SANCTIFICATION

The positional reality of sanctification is the first reference point the Bible provides to keep us on a safe trajectory. When we consider what the Bible has to say about our spiritual growth, we must recognize that there is an aspect of sanctification that is positional and definite rather than progressive and manifold. In positional terms, the Bible speaks of Christians as already sanctified. This means that as much as we need to grow in our sanctification, we do not need to grow into it. Sanctification is not frequently considered in these terms, but it should be, because when the positional reality of sanctification is neglected, a significant portion of what the Bible teaches about this doctrine is overlooked.

A new position

First Corinthians 6:9-11 serves as a specific example of the NT's teaching on the positional reality of sanctification:

> Or do you not know that the unrighteous will not inherit the kingdom of God? Do not be deceived: neither the sexually immoral, nor idolaters, nor adulterers, nor men who practice homosexuality, nor thieves, nor the greedy, nor drunkards, nor revilers, nor swindlers will inherit the kingdom of God. And such were some of you. But you were washed, you were sanctified, you were justified in the name of the Lord Jesus Christ and by the Spirit of our God.

Paul provides a stark contrast between the believer's former life of unrighteousness and their present condition in salvation. He does not hesitate, even with reference to the worldly Corinthians, to speak of washing, sanctification, and justification in the exact same manner. Each term highlights a distinct aspect of salvation, but also represents a present reality for the believer, including sanctification.

We have been set apart—consecrated to God—through the work of Christ. His death not only secures our justification; it makes our sanctification a reality. The full extent of our sanctification has not yet occurred, so we look forward to the time when "he who began a good work in [us] will complete it" (Phil 1:6) and present us "in splendor, without spot or wrinkle" (Eph

5:27). However, this does not change the fact that Christ has definitively sanctified us. We are not yet what we will be when our sanctification is complete, but our present position guarantees the future results.

A holy position

The positional reality of sanctification is further demonstrated by the NT use of the term "saint", which literally means "holy one." Sainthood has nothing to do with Catholic veneration or a higher level of holiness. The NT always has ordinary Christians in view when it uses this designation (1 Cor 1:1; Rom 1:1; Phil 1:1), because every believer has been consecrated by God unto holiness. The call of God (Eph 1:4) and the work of Christ have set apart the entire church, not just an elite group of Christians within the church. We can rest assured that our sainthood does not depend on the veneration of man, but rests in the victory of Christ.

Positional holiness does not negate the need for personal holiness. Christ positionally and practically makes us His "holy ones," which means that the positional reality of our sanctification affects the practical reality of our lives. Our sainthood doesn't depend upon our fruit, but it will produce fruit in us. The NT consistently presents these two concepts in the same breath. Ephesians 5:3 says that "sexual immorality and all impurity or covetousness must not even be named among you, as is proper among saints." In other words, there is a proper manner of life that is made possible by our definitive sanctification. This is great news for us because it means that saints no longer live under the reign of sin. We are no longer bound by and tethered to transgression. We have been set apart by grace and freed for righteousness (Romans 6:1-14). So, whether you are battling sin or confessing it, the positional reality of your sanctification fuels your pursuit of holiness. Too often we lose sight of this pivotal reference point.

THE PROGRESSIVE RESPONSIBILITY OF SANCTIFICATION

The second reference point the Bible provides to keep Christians on a safe trajectory is the progressive responsibility of sanctification. Positional sanctification is always for a purpose. The elements of the temple were sanctified by God so that they could serve a specific function in the worship of the Lord. So too, we have been positionally sanctified so that we can worship the Lord with our lives. In other words, the Holy Spirit set us apart through regeneration so that we could ever-increasingly serve and follow Christ. This positional work of the Holy Spirit always has an ongoing and sanctifying effect in our lives.

Progressive growth

In a sense, positional sanctification is the counterpart to total depravity. Depravity pervaded our hearts with the controlling influence of sin while we were in Adam. But now that we are in Christ, the Holy Spirit dwells in our hearts, permeating us with the controlling influence of holiness. Positional sanctification does not mean that we become as holy as we could be. It means that every area of our life is now under the influence of the sanctifying Spirit. We are totally set apart, but not yet completely holy. Thus, there is a continuing need for progressive sanctification.

One of the clearest proofs of the progressive nature of sanctification is found in 2 Corinthians 3:18, "And we all, with unveiled face, beholding the glory of the Lord, are being transformed into the same image from one degree of glory to another. For this comes from the Lord who is the Spirit." Twice in this verse alone Paul refers to the progress of sanctification. First, Paul uses the word μεταμορφόω (metamorphoō), which is translated "being transformed." Like the English descendant of this word (metamorphosis), the Greek term refers to a fundamental change. Paul does not speak of this change in definite or positional terms, but uses the present tense to depict the unfolding reality of this transformation. It is a change that has already taken place, and yet it continues to take place. Interestingly, Paul uses the same word and verb tense in Romans 12:2 when he commands Christians to "be transformed by the renewal of your mind." In other words, not only should we expect progress in the Christian life; we are commanded to pursue this progress.

Back in 1 Corinthians 3:18, Paul also explains that this transformation transports us from "one degree of glory to another." With this language, "Paul's point is that through the Spirit we are able now to live a more Christ-like life… and to bring greater glory to God."[10] The Spirit is conforming us to the glorious image of Christ—this is the essence of progressive sanctification. We were predestined to be made holy like Christ, and God is progressively working every detail of our life toward that end (Rom 8:29).

Every Christian should be able to perceive this process in their own life. Sure, there are times when growth is imperceptible, or we even feel like we are moving backwards. But when we examine the overall trajectory of our Christian lives, there should be a trend toward maturity. Your sanctification

---

[10] David E. Garland, *2 Corinthians*. Vol. 29. NAC (Nashville: Broadman & Holman Publishers, 1999), 201.

should be producing growth, maturity, and spiritual progress in your life. You can probably remember a time when you were a babe in the faith, surviving on milk. But I hope that doesn't describe you anymore. If you have been a Christian your whole life, and you can only digest the milk of the faith, that is a problem. If you are not experiencing growth, it may be because you are not fulfilling your responsibilities in sanctification.

Progressive effort

God does not leave us alone in our spiritual growth. "The Holy Spirit acts in sanctification to unite us to Christ, constitute us as God's saints, and begin the lifelong process of making us holy."[11] We have the Spirit, we have grace, and we have the power of Christ at work within us. All of this means that God is ultimately responsible for our growth in sanctification. However, God does not automatically mature us. He uses means to accomplish this purpose, and one of those means is our active participation. Not only is the Christian life characterized by growth, it is also characterized by our participation in that growth. The progressive nature of our sanctification creates a responsibility for us. We are "duty bound to strive for ever-increasing sanctification by using the means which God has placed at [our] disposal."[12]

To some, this might sound inconsistent with the concept of grace, but words like "duty," "strive," "work," and other similar imperatives litter the pages of the NT:

- Brothers, I do not consider that I have made it my own. But one thing I do: forgetting what lies behind and **straining forward** to what lies ahead, I **press on** toward the goal for the prize of the upward call of God in Christ Jesus. (Phil 3:13–14)

- For if you live according to the flesh you will die, but if by the Spirit you **put to death the deeds of the body**, you will live. (Rom 8:13)

- And everyone who thus hopes in him **purifies himself** as he is pure. (1 Jn 3:3)

---

[11] Robert A. Peterson, *Salvation Applied by the Spirit: Union with Christ* (Wheaton, IL: Crossway Books, 2015), 337.

[12] Louis Berkhof, *Systematic Theology* (Grand Rapids: W.B. Eerdmans Pub. Co, 1996), 534.

- In your **struggle** against sin you have not yet **resisted** to the point of shedding your blood. (Heb 12:4)

- Since we have these promises, beloved, let us **cleanse ourselves** from every defilement of body and spirit, bringing holiness to completion in the fear of God. (2 Cor 7:1)

- For this very reason, **make every effort** to supplement your faith with virtue, and virtue with knowledge… .(2 Pt 1:5)

- Do you not know that in a race all the runners run, but only one receives the prize? So **run that you may obtain it.** (1 Cor 9:24)

- You therefore, beloved, knowing this beforehand, **take care** that you are not carried away with the error of lawless people and lose your own stability. But **grow** in the grace and knowledge of our Lord and Savior Jesus Christ. To him be the glory both now and to the day of eternity. Amen. (2 Pt 3:17–18)

- …so as to walk in a manner worthy of the Lord, fully pleasing to him, **bearing fruit in every good work** and increasing in the knowledge of God. (Colossians 1:10)

- Show yourself in all respects to **be a model of good works**, and in your teaching show integrity, dignity…. (Tit 2:7)

- …Who gave himself for us to redeem us from all lawlessness and to purify for himself a people for his own possession who are **zealous for good work**s. (Tit 2:14)

The authors of the NT had no problem speaking of our role in sanctification in these terms, and if the Holy Spirit didn't hesitate to use them, then neither should we. We need to explain them carefully and to understand them within the context of saving and enabling grace, but it is not illegitimate to speak of the Christian's duty in progressive sanctification. We have an obligation to put forth effort in our sanctification, and this responsibility does not contradict gospel grace—it celebrates the grace that enables victory over sin.

Since Christians are responsible to take an active role in their sanctification, it is helpful to gain clarity on what this looks like in practice. Although much could be said about the believer's role in sanctification, our responsibility in sanctification can essentially be summarized in three words: meditation, mortification, and vivification.

Meditation

Consider, first of all, meditation. This, of course, is not referring to some type of mind-emptying behavior. Instead, it is speaking of the exact opposite. Thomas Manton defined meditation as "that duty or exercise of religion whereby the mind is applied to the serious and solemn contemplation of spiritual things, for practical uses and purposes."[13] In other words, biblical meditation is taking the time and making the effort to consider the implications of God's truth for your life. As Christians, we have a responsibility to fill our minds with the knowledge of Scripture and to bring our way of thinking under the authority of God's truth.

Meditating—thinking deeply about the Bible—plays a crucial role in the Christian life. In fact, Colossians 1:10 directly links growth in knowledge with growth in sanctification: "walk in a manner worthy of the Lord, fully pleasing to him, bearing fruit in every good work and increasing in the knowledge of God." Increased understanding of the truth is required for fruit-bearing maturity, but the truth will not penetrate the depths of your heart until you meditate on the depth of the truth. If we are going to fulfill our responsibility to grow in Christ, we must permeate our thinking with the truth about Christ.

Mortification

Meditation always leads to mortification. As we increasingly fill our minds with the glory of God, we will increasingly desire to mortify the sin that falls short of God's glory. What is mortification? John Owen, author of the *The Mortification of Sin*, explains that "to 'mortify' means to put any living thing to death. To kill a man, or any other living thing, is to take away the principle of all its strength, vigor, and power, so that it cannot act, or exert or put forth any proper actings of its own."[14] In other words, to mortify means to kill, which is what we must do to the sinful inclinations that plague us from within.

---

[13] Thomas Manton, *The Works of Thomas Manton,* vol. 17, "Sermons Upon Genesis 24:63" (Worthington, PA: Maranatha Publications, 1979) 267.

[14] John Owen, *The Mortification of Sin* (Carlisle, PA: Banner of Truth Trust, 2004), 3.

Colossians 3:5 commands, "Put to death therefore what is earthly in you: sexual immorality, impurity, passion, evil desire, and covetousness, which is idolatry." To this Owen adds, "You must be always at it while you live; do not take a day off from this work; always be killing sin or it will be killing you."[15] Remaining sin perpetually schemes against growth in godliness, which is why we must be ever-vigilant to mortify every sin that separates us from God. "Not for a moment…dare we delude ourselves into thinking that the victory will be won consistently without blood, sweat, and tears. Surviving sin…is not reigning sin, but it is real sin."[16] We must battle sin with the power that Christ provides. As Romans 13:14 teaches, "Put on the Lord Jesus Christ, and make no provision for the flesh, to gratify its desires." Mortification demands that we starve sin to death, so we feed on the person of Christ.

The work of mortification acknowledges the inner workings of the human heart, including the insatiable desire for carnal gratification. Without the help of the Holy Spirit, sinful man would always choose the gratification of lust over the mortification of sin—to feed the flesh rather than to starve the flesh. There is a universal temptation among all sinners to protect the possibility for gratification, even if they don't indulge in it. The flesh is frequently willing to wait on gratification, but it cannot stand the thought of losing the opportunity for gratification altogether. It is OK with shutting the door on sin as long as the keys to the door are kept nearby. Thus, there is an internal battle within every believer to completely cut off every resource, opportunity, and encouragement to sin that remains in our lives. The only way to decrease the intensity of this battle is to put on new life in Christ and put to death the sinful appetites of the old life.

Vivification

If mortification describes a negative aspect of our responsibility, then vivification is the positive aspect. Mortification is the active movement away from sin, and vivification is the active movement toward the newness of life we have in Christ. Ephesians 4:23-24 captures the idea from an inspired perspective. "…To put off your old self, which belongs to your former manner of life and is corrupt through deceitful desires, and to be renewed in the spirit of your minds, and to put on the new self, created after the likeness of God in true righteousness and holiness." The point is that we have been made alive, and we need to walk in this newness of life.

---

[15] *Ibid.*, 5.

[16] Sinclair Ferguson, *The Christian Life: A Doctrinal Introduction* (Carlisle, PA: Banner of Truth, 1989), 157.

Sanctification does not consist only of staying away from sin; it requires following the Spirit's leading unto righteousness. We must weed out the sin from the garden of our hearts, and cultivate the soil to produce healthy fruit. Both are required and always work together to produce a life of repentance. To put off and put on means to mortify and vivify, and the two concepts jointly define the work of repentance, which is at the heart of our responsibility in sanctification. True spiritual growth never takes place without true spiritual repentance.

Repentance is a change to your life stemming from a change in your mind. The importance of repentance does not fade away after a believer's initial conversion. In fact, the Christian life can be characterized largely by the work of repentance. Conversely, many of the spiritual problems Christians face can be traced back to a lack of repentance, or, at least, a superficial repentance. Many have confused worldly sorrow (2 Cor 7:10) with genuine repentance, which is why they do not see the fruit of change in their lives. A sorrow that leads to repentance possesses spiritual value, but a sorrow focused solely on worldly ramifications—such as embarrassment, regret, distaste for the consequences of sin, etc.—will only lead to the same sins over and over again. This is why it is crucial for believers to examine the repentance in their lives and make sure it is a godly and thorough repentance.

Repentance must be godly in the sense that it is Godward in focus. That is to say, true repentance recognizes that sin is ultimately against God and must be dealt with before God. Repentance must be thorough in the sense that it is penetrating in depth. True repentance recognizes that sin is an issue of the heart and must be dealt with at a heart level. The thoroughness of genuine repentance is usually where individuals stumble. Upon seeing sin in their life, they are willing to show remorse for sinning against God, confess it to God, and seek forgiveness from God. However, when it comes to rooting through the recesses of their hearts to determine the underlying unbelief and lustful allegiances that caused the sin, few are willing to go that far. As a result of superficial repentance, their fruit is often superficial as well.

Thorough repentance won't happen without a battle, it won't always be pretty, and it is usually painstakingly hard. At the same time, however, you can be confident that thorough repentance won't happen without fruit. The sweetest fruits of the Christian life are cultivated through godly and thorough repentance.

These three words—meditation, mortification and vivification—encapsulate our responsibility in progressive sanctification:

- **_Meditation:_** utilizing your new capacity fill your mind with truth (Col 1:10).
- **_Mortification:_** utilizing your new capacity to kill sin (Col 3:5; Rom 13:14).
- **_Vivification:_** utilizing your new capacity to pursue righteousness (1 Tim 6:11)

By faith we must seek to fulfill these responsibilities. As just stated, it won't always be pretty and it is usually painstakingly hard, but we have God's help. His grace enlists us in our own sanctification, not out of necessity but as opportunity. We can strive in these areas knowing that our salvation doesn't depend on our performance, that we have the grace we need to be effective, and that God has promised to use this effort for our growth.

THE PERFECT REALIZATION OF SANCTIFICATION

There is one final reference point the Bible provides to keep us on a right trajectory in our understanding of sanctification. Our positional reality and progressive responsibility will one day culminate in the perfect realization of sanctification. What definite sanctification secures, and progressive sanctification refines, perfected sanctification will one day attain. This is also known as glorification, when we will be raised with Christ and "made conformable to His own glorious body."[17] Glorification is the eschatological fulfillment of our sanctification.

Future realization

Some have argued that the completion of our sanctification can take place on earth and that a higher holiness, or Christian perfection, is possible. This certainly would have been a surprise to the apostle John, who said in 1 John 1:10 that "if we say we have not sinned, we make him a liar, and his word is not in us." John's words provide the death knell for the perfectionist position. The possibility of perfection in this life is simply inconsistent with God's truth. Our citizenship is in heaven with Christ, and Philippians 3:21 says that is where He "will transform our lowly body to be like his glorious body, by the power that enables him even to subject all things to himself."

---

[17] _The Westminster Confession of Faith, XXXII.iii._

Guaranteed realization

Christians will not experience perfection in this age, but their perfection in the age to come is guaranteed. We can be confident that faithfulness in this life will be graciously rewarded not because it is worthy of God, but because God graciously promised to reward it. Moreover, the failures compiled in this age will dissipate in the light of God's glorious grace when we will be enveloped in our union with Christ (1 Cor 15:50-54). What does an eternity of perfected sanctification mean for a Christians battling for incremental progress in sanctification? 1 Corinthians 15:58 answers the question: "Therefore, my beloved brothers, be steadfast, immovable, always abounding in the work of the Lord, knowing that in the Lord your labor is not in vain." Faithful effort in sanctification is never in vain, because we have a sure hope that God will use every ordained means to perfect His work in us, including our effort. The perfect realization of our sanctification should embolden us to continue moving forward on a biblical trajectory toward our ultimate hope.

CONCLUSION

The safe return of Apollo 13 motivated the astronauts to continue working despite extreme difficulty. But their homecoming depended on the right trajectory—devastation loomed with any deviation. In order to stay on trajectory, the astronauts had to perform several manual burns of the engine without their normal navigational instruments. During these engine burns there was only one way for them to stay on course: they had to find reference points out the window of the lunar module. In the transcript of the flight logs, Commander Jim Lovell described what he had to do in order to stay on the precise trajectory: "What I'm going to do is…stop with the Earth in the commander's window…and then I'm going to maneuver the spacecraft so that I have the lighted portion of the Earth at the top of the window."[18] Using the earth as a reference point, the astronauts were able to keep the lunar module on the only safe trajectory, which ultimately got them home safely.

---

[18] The full transcript of this incredible recording can be accessed at http://apollo13.spacelog.org/page/03:14:37:36/, viewed on 2.2.15.

When it comes to the doctrine of sanctification, there is only one safe trajectory to get us where we need to go–a biblical trajectory. The Apollo 13 astronauts used heavenly bodies to navigate their way home, and we have heavenly truth to do the same thing. The only way to stay on a safe trajectory in sanctification is to keep our sights on the biblical reference points God has provided for us.

4
THE MECHANICS OF SANCTIFICATION

I don't put together many puzzles, and when I do, it's usually with my two-year-old daughter, which means there are only about twelve very large pieces. Really, that's about all I can handle when it comes to puzzles. My dad, on the other hand, loves puzzles. I vividly remember our entire family working on massive puzzles with tiny pieces spread across the kitchen table. For days we would pick away at it until, finally, the last wispy cloud or tree branch completed a pastoral landscape. Along the way, we always followed dad's sage puzzle solving strategy: start with the corner pieces, move to the edges, and use the picture on the box to help you fill in the middle. The strategy certainly did not originate with my dad, but I learned it from watching him. But every once-in-a-while dad would ignore his own strategy and assemble the puzzle face-down for an extra challenge. Whenever I saw him fitting together cardboard colored puzzle pieces, I always steered clear of the kitchen table. I already have a low tolerance for the tediousness of puzzles, but there is nothing more frustrating than working on a puzzle without the picture. You don't know where you are going, how all the pieces fit together, or where your next move will be. You are trying to make progress without any reference point and without any way of building on your success. It is an exasperating experience that mirrors what many Christians feel as they seek to grow in grace.

I fear that many Christians are trying to put the puzzle of sanctification together upside down. My dad intentionally ignored the proper mechanics of puzzle solving to create a challenge for himself, but many Christians have unintentionally made their spiritual growth more challenging than it needs to be because they do not understand the practical mechanics of sanctification. In many corners of evangelicalism, the ignorance stems from a lack of teaching. Christians have been cut off from the sanctifying resources promised in the Bible because they have never heard of them. Spiritual growth is a mystery that, for many, remains unexplained. Some Christians grow rapidly, others do not, and neither knows why. Progress becomes enigmatic, stumbling becomes expected, and the process of sanctification, designed to be edifying, becomes exasperating. In desperation, Christians look elsewhere to fill the void left by this lack of instruction. Sometimes they look for answers from within, and other times they seek direction from the world around them. Either way, it's not pretty. Instead of proven biblical strategies for spiritual maturation, visceral impulses and worldly pragmatism chart the course of sanctification. Along the way, there are no reference points to make sure they are heading in the right direction, except "if it feels right it must be working."

Thankfully, the solution to the problem is simple: we need to turn the puzzle right side up. The Bible paints a detailed picture of what sanctification looks like, and we need to start referring to that picture to put the pieces of our spiritual life together. How do we do that? We begin by admonishing Christians to abandon unbiblical and "abiblical" models of growth, and to accept what the Bible says about spiritual maturity. The wisdom of this world will never produce the sanctification of God because, as 1 Corinthians 3:19 reminds us, "the wisdom of this world is folly with God." Christians who ape the self-help techniques, pop psychology, and sentimental spirituality of this age should not expect progress in sanctification.

Spiritual maturity flows from understanding and appropriating biblical truth. If we want to see growth in our lives, we need to identify the biblical mechanics of sanctification. What are these mechanics of sanctification? They can be boiled down to four essential components: grace (*the cause)*, truth (*the catalyst*), faith (*the channel*) and worship (*the culmination*). Or, to put it another way, God's grace is the source of our sanctification, biblical truth is the means of our sanctification, growing faith is our responsibility in sanctification, and a life of worship is the result of sanctification. When God's people understand these practical components of the Christian life, sanctification comes alive.

THE CAUSE: GRACE

The mechanics of sanctification begin with God's unmerited grace, which is the ultimate cause of sanctification. The process of spiritual growth does not elevate us above the need for grace; it plunges us deeper into the storehouses of grace in the pursuit of holiness. Since we can't sanctify ourselves, any talk about progress, growth, or maturation must occur in the context of grace. Sanctification is built upon a foundation of grace with materials provided by grace. The better we understand this provision, the better equipped we will be to grow in sanctifying grace. What must we understand about this grace?

A grace to rest in

For starters, in the course of everyday life, every believer needs to understand that they can *rest* in the grace God provides for sanctification. At this point it might help to define grace. Grace is not a substance that we must find on our own or that we can manipulate by our works. Grace is the *kind disposition of God toward unworthy man.* It is the ever-present help of God for those who do not deserve it (Ps 46:1). Thus, to say that sanctification requires grace is to say that sanctification requires the kindness of God's undeserved help. We can rest in this grace, in part, because it is unmerited. Perfect love is what motives sovereign grace, and there is nothing the believer could do to foil the loving purposes of the King of Creation (1 Pet 1:3-5). In other words, we cannot fall from God's grace, because we did not ascend to it. Additionally, we do not need to doubt this grace, because it was made sure for us through Christ. God called us into a grace that Christ won on our behalf. Every blessing that flows from the "Fount of every blessing" has been secured for us by Christ; we have been blessed with every spiritual blessing *in Christ* (Eph 1:3).

Even amid the trials and temptations of this life, you can be "sure of this, that he who began a good work in you will bring it to completion at the day of Jesus Christ" (Phil 1:6). When you stumble and fall, you don't have to hide it for fear of losing grace, because "if we confess our sins, he is faithful and just to forgive us our sins and to cleanse us from all unrighteousness" (1 Jn 1:9). In the battle of Romans 7—when you do what you don't want to do and don't do what you know you should—you can exult in the comfort of Romans 8:1, which says "there is therefore now no condemnation for those who are in Christ Jesus." In fact, the believer can rest in the entirety of Romans 8, which promises in verses 31-39 that nothing can separate us from grace of God found in Christ:

> What then shall we say to these things? If God is for us, who can be against us? He who did not spare his own Son but gave him up for us all, how will he not also with him graciously give us all things? Who shall bring any charge against God's elect? It is God who justifies. Who is to condemn? Christ Jesus is the one who died—more than that, who was raised—who is at the right hand of God, who indeed is interceding for us. Who shall separate us from

the love of Christ? Shall tribulation, or distress, or persecution, or famine, or nakedness, or danger, or sword? As it is written, "For your sake we are being killed all the day long; we are regarded as sheep to be slaughtered." No, in all these things we are more than conquerors through him who loved us. For I am sure that neither death nor life, nor angels nor rulers, nor things present nor things to come, nor powers, nor height nor depth, nor anything else in all creation, will be able to separate us from the love of God in Christ Jesus our Lord. (Romans 8:31-39)

The Father's eternal love for the Christian is just as sure as His love for Christ, and His permanent grace makes us conquerors despite our sin. This is the context in which the fight for sanctification takes place, and this grace is the only true source of spiritual rest.

A grace to run in

As glorious as these truths are, they only begin to describe the grace we have for sanctification. God's grace also transforms us from within and retrofits us for the process of spiritual growth, which means that just as surely as we can rest in grace, so too, we can run in the grace God provides for sanctification. MacArthur is absolutely correct when he points out that, "grace does not change a person's standing before God yet leave his character untouched."[19] Titus 2:11-14 confirms that the same grace that saves us from unrighteousness trains us in righteousness:

> For the grace of God has appeared, bringing salvation for all people, training us to renounce ungodliness and worldly passions, and to live self-controlled, upright, and godly lives in the present age, waiting for our blessed hope, the appearing of the glory of our great God and Savior Jesus Christ, who gave himself for us to redeem us from all lawlessness and to purify for himself a people for his own possession who are zealous for good works.

Did you catch what Paul is saying here? The same gospel grace that brings salvation to the sinner also trains the saint for holiness. The word "trains" can mean "disciplines," which is how it is translated in Hebrews 12:6: "For the Lord disciplines the one he loves, and chastises every son whom he receives." Grace does not merely forgive us of our sin; it empowers us to renounces the remaining influences of sin in our lives. To put it another

---

[19] John MacArthur, *The Gospel According to Jesus,* Revised and Expanded Anniversary Edition (Grand Rapids: Zondervan Publishing, 2008) 46.

way, God's abounding grace sufficiently supplies us with what we need to abound in good works, and it compels us to pursue those good works (2 Cor 9:8). The same grace that secures us in Christ also sustains us as we seek to obediently follow Christ. As John Owen so succinctly reminds us, "we cannot perform our duty without the grace of God; nor does God give his grace for any other purpose than that we may perform our duty."[20] The grace of God initiated by the Father's election, accomplished through the work of the Son, and applied by the ministry of Holy Spirit always accomplishes its purpose, and in the case of sanctification, that purpose is to make us holy. Grace is the ultimate cause of spiritual growth.

THE CATALYST: TRUTH

The mechanics of sanctification begin with God's unmerited grace, which includes God's revealed truth. Truth is the primary tool He uses to make us holy. God does not secretly or mysteriously mature us. He has chosen to use means to supply us with the sanctifying grace that we need on a daily basis. These means of grace are the divine instruments designed to form us into "his workmanship, created in Christ Jesus for good works, which God prepared beforehand, that we should walk in them" (Eph 2:10). God does not inexplicably zap us into conformity to Christ. He uses identifiable instruments over time to do this work. It is not necessary for God to use external instruments like the Bible, prayer, church and the ordinances to make us like Jesus, but I am glad that He did. Because God has chosen to use ordinary means of grace to make us holy, it is possible for us to know where to go for the grace that we need daily. The more we pattern our lives around these graces, and the longer we endure under these sanctifying disciplines, the deeper our dependence upon and trust in God will become. As a result, we can humbly participate in practical spiritual disciplines with the assurance that God will use them to fortify our faith.

The grace of truth

When it comes to the means of grace, the Bible is the preeminent means of sanctifying grace. Actually, all other means of grace benefit us only insofar as they relate to biblical truth. For instance, prayer must be rooted in the promises and priorities of the Bible in order to benefit our souls. So too, the ordinances must proclaim and point to divine truth to have a sanctifying effect. There is no such thing as a means of grace that is detached from

---

[20] John Owen "Discourse on the Holy Spirit," The Works of John Owen, Vol. 3, ed. William H. Gould, 384.

biblical truth—the truth of God's Word is always the catalyst for spiritual growth.

Think of it this way—no one desires your sanctification more than Jesus. In fact, he spent his final hours on earth praying, among other things, for your sanctification. Notice that when Jesus prayed for your spiritual growth in John 17:17, He knew that growth would take place in you because of the truth's influence on your life: "Sanctify them in the truth; your word is truth." Jesus not only interceded for our sanctification; He expected it to happen as a result of God's Word. Jesus was confident that the Author of truth graciously sanctifies His people with the truth.

We find the same priority of truth in Ephesians 5:27, where it speaks of the work Christ accomplished for the church so that He "might sanctify her, having cleansed her by the washing of water *with the word,* so that he might present the church to himself in splendor, without spot or wrinkle or any such thing, that she might be holy and without blemish." Here we see that the work of Christ only becomes effective unto sanctification in connection with the Word of God. Notice how this worked for the disciples in John 15:3 where Jesus says, "Already you are clean because of the word that I have spoken to you." The disciples were already benefitting from the cleansing work of Christ, but only because the truth of His Word had been revealed to them. To put it in theological terms, the work objectively accomplished by Christ is subjectively applied to us through the instrument of the truth.

The authority of truth

To put it more simply, Christ uses truth to sanctify His people. This is a crucial principle to recognize because it means suppressing the truth stunts growth, and submitting to the truth stimulates growth. This simple principle acts as a lynchpin for the practical mechanics of sanctification. If grace is the ultimate cause of our sanctification, then truth is the instrumental cause which cultivates our maturity. God's truth confronts our sinful thinking, challenges the lies we are tempted to believe, and commands us to submit our will to the Lordship of Christ. As we bring our lives—every thought, belief, and action—under the authority of Scripture, the Spirit is conforming us to the image of Christ. In other words, *the Spirit of God uses the Word of God to sanctify the people of God.* The Bible is what produces the faith convictions we need to live lives of holiness; truth is the Spirit's catalyst to ignite our hearts for growth.

THE CHANNEL: FAITH

Understanding the importance of grace and truth in our spiritual growth leaves us with the question: what part does the Christian play in sanctification? The answer is that believers participate in their own sanctification primarily through faith. Faith is the channel by which God's people receive God's grace and benefit from God's truth; if you don't believe God you won't yield to His grace or His truth. From start to finish, the Christian life must be lived by faith. *Through faith*, the believer is united with Christ unto justification, and through faith the believer benefits from a restored relationship with Christ for sanctification. *Through faith*, new life in Christ is initiated and daily life in Christ is sustained. *Through faith*, we are brought into union with Christ, and *through faith* we benefit from our communion with Christ. God designed the Christian life to be a life of faith, which is why faith summarizes our responsibility in sanctification. In the words of the apostle Paul, "we walk by faith, not by sight" (2 Corinthians 5:7).

The fight for faith

To be clear, faith does not merit grace nor self-generate growth. Ultimately, the only reason we have faith is because God had mercy on us. Faith is a gift which has been instilled in us. It led to our salvation, and it provides us with the channel we need to funnel God's sustaining grace into our life. This faith, initiated by God through regeneration, is designed to increase through progressive sanctification. Progressive sanctification hinges on the reality that where faith abounds, so does maturity. Jesus explicitly states in Acts 26:18 that believers "are sanctified by faith in me." This is true of positional sanctification and of growth in progressive sanctification. Christians are set apart unto God through faith, and they mature in their walk with God through faith.

The fight for sanctification is really a fight for faith; if we want to increase in personal holiness, we need to increasingly respond to our circumstances with faith. This is not always easy. It is often a struggle to believe in the midst of the day-to-day grind and the overwhelming trials of life. In fact, all Christians will see a reflection of their own spiritual life in the father who cries out in Mark 9:24, "I believe; help my unbelief." This is one of the truest and purest confessions in the entire Bible, and it describes every individual in the process of sanctification. It also demonstrates the need for increasing faith to face life. Not faith in faith, but faith in Jesus as the gracious giver of faith. More and more we need to accept and appropriate

His promises and precepts in our everyday lives if we want to see spiritual growth.

The fruits of faith

The priority of faith doesn't preclude the presence of works (James 2:14-26), nor does it negate our obligation to pursue obedience (Phil 2:12). God has called us to diligently pursue righteousness as an outworking of our faith. This means that all of our good works must pass through the channel of faith springing from our believing hearts. This means that we must seek to grow our faith if we want to grow in holiness. Increasing faith causes the soil of our heart to be fertile for growth, and the growing fruit in our lives needs to be characterized by ongoing faith. Hebrews 11:6 teaches us that any effort employed in sanctification must traverse the channel of faith to be pleasing to God: "Without faith it is impossible to please God." As we will see, our sanctification is ultimately about pleasing God, which cannot be done apart from trusting Him. Good works aren't good, meaningful worship isn't meaningful, and genuine service isn't genuine without faith. So, for instance, there may be times in the Christian life when it is appropriate to weep instead of rejoicing (Rom 12:15), or to mourn instead of feeling joy (James 4:9), or to be convicted rather than comforted (2 Cor 7:10), but there is never a moment when it is unnecessary to believe God.

Faith is the key to our pursuit of growth, because genuine faith is what distinguishes between legalistic effort and gospel obedience. To be clear, moralism isn't striving too hard; it is striving without faith. Jesus labored to the point of exhaustion to do the will of the Father—that wasn't legalistic. Paul worked night and day in order to serve the church—he wasn't reverting back to his ways as a Pharisee. Diligent labor, toilsome work, and strenuous efforts aren't the signs of legalism; they are frequently the fruits of faith. The root of legalism is *faithless* effort, not too much effort. Unbelieving works will always produce the fruit of self-righteous, self-willed, self-justifying pride. When you get to the heart of the matter, legalism replaces humble dependence on Christ will rebellious pride. If the Christian life is hard for you, that doesn't make you a Pharisee. If you are serving out of unbelieving pride rather than faith-filled worship, that's contrary to the gospel.

All of our efforts toward spiritual growth must come back to our trust in God and our belief in His word. Faith is the mediate cause of sanctification; it is how man participates in the divine miracle of making sinners holy. This means that growth in godliness will require you to trust the God who freely gives His grace and clearly revealed His truth. Sanctification requires us to be good stewards of the faith God instilled in us by informing, increasing, and implementing it. This is our primary responsibility as disciples—we must take the ten talents God has entrusted us with, and seek to increase them for His glory (Matt 25:14-30).

THE CULMINATION: WORSHIP

The result of grace, truth, and faith will always be worship, which is the culmination of sanctification. The process that begins with the grace of God ends with the glory of God. It makes perfect sense that God would sanctify us for His glory, since that is what he created us for. In other words, if the glory of God is the chief end of man,[21] then it certainly must be the chief end of the sanctified man. This means that if we think about sanctification in a manner that does not give God glory, we are thinking wrongly. At the same time, if the manner in which we live out our sanctification does not result in the glory of God, we are living wrongly. Worship is the goal of the Christian life, and sanctification is uniquely worshipful because it glorifies God to transform sinners, and transformed sinners always glorify God.

Sanctified for worship

Worship is an important piece in the puzzle of sanctification, especially if we want to understand the relationship between positional and progressive sanctification. God sets us apart positionally so that we can worship Him. Just as the vessels in the OT temple were sanctified in the sense that they were set apart for worship, we are set apart for holy service to God. Christians are definitively reconstituted in Christ for God's glory. Progressively, God continues to sanctify us, conforming us to the image of Christ, so that we can more effectively offer Him holy and acceptable worship. Thus, worship is the purpose of both progressive and positional sanctification (Romans 12:1-2). This truth has some very practical implications for the Christian life. For instance, as God progressively sanctifies you, you increasingly prioritize Him. As a result of God's grace in the process of sanctification, our love for and obedience to God's Word become faith-driven acts of worship. We are not acting to earn God's favor or manipulate His blessings. Instead, we perform these duties out of a heart of worship for the God who has lavished His grace upon us. God makes us holy in order to make us worshipers.

---

[21] See the Westminster Confession

Sanctified by worship

In addition to being the result of sanctification, worship also plays a key role in producing sanctification. One of the means of grace God uses to make us holy is worship, which is the ultimate motivation for our effort in sanctification. Think about it from a divine perspective. God's chief aim is to glorify His holy name in all that He does, including salvation (Ezek 36:22-24). The proliferation of His own glory is the preeminent purpose of His sanctifying work. If this is the divine motivation for sanctification, it should be our primary motive as well. We should be driven to glorify our God through our actions and attitudes. Our job and our joy should be to make the name of our God great. We could certainly come up with other legitimate motivations from the Scriptures; however, unless all of these motivators flow through the filter of worship, we run the risk of turning our sanctification into a man-centered endeavor. If I put forth effort in sanctification *only* to be more mature, satisfied, and joyful, or to fulfill my obligation, then my motives contradict God's motives. This is not to say that I won't benefit in these ways from sanctification, or that these motives are sinful. However, the ultimate goal of my maturity, sanctification, good works, and personal joy is God's glory. Too many Christians languish in a stagnant spiritual life simply because they have been pursuing sanctification for selfish purposes. Worship is the key because it is the duty and the delight of the Christian life. This is why God designed sanctification to be permeated by and to culminate in worship. In other words, God is most glorified in us when we are most sanctified by Him.

CONCLUSION

Grace, truth, faith, worship—these are the key components God uses to glorify Himself and to sanctify His people. Grace is the source of sanctification, truth drives sanctification, faith receives sanctification, and worship realizes sanctification. You don't have to languish in confusion or muddle through obscurity in your Christian life. You don't have to wonder why sometimes you grow and other times you fail. And you certainly don't have to look to the world for paradigms of growth.

By faith, you can receive the grace and truth that you need to live a worshipful life to the God who saved your soul. Spiritual growth won't always be easy, but you'll know how it is designed to work. Every time you face the decision to choose gratification over mortification, it will be a battle of faith with lasting spiritual implications. In those moments, you can rely on God's grace, seek His truth, trust what He commands, and worship

Him by killing even the seeds of sin in your life. This is what sanctification looks like in real time. From time to time you might get frustrated with your growth, but you don't have to be frustrated with God's design. The process of sanctification isn't simple, but the plan is clear. Don't turn the puzzle face-down, and don't ignore the perfect paradigm God has provided in Scripture. If you understand these mechanics, then you have the picture you need to put the puzzle of sanctification together.

5
THE GRACE OF PREACHING

Martyn Lloyd-Jones once declared "without any hesitation that the most urgent need in the Christian Church today is true preaching."[22] This prescription from "The Doctor" rings true for the church as a whole and for the individual Christian as well. Preaching is not only the greatest need in the church, it is the most powerful resource for sanctification in the life of every believer. No personal discipline, new strategy, or life-changing experience can rival the power of preaching for sanctification, and it is not even close. *Biblical preaching is the primary means of grace for sanctification.*

As I previously asked, how many mature Christians do you know that have not been heavily influenced by faithful preaching? Again, if you are anything like me, the answer is none. In fact, it was this observation that drove me toward this study. In my own church, I noticed that the most effective servants and encouraging members were the ones inundating themselves with faithful teaching. As I began to recognize the correlation between preaching and maturity within my own congregation, I went to the Scriptures and found the exact same pattern. In both my pastoral experience and on the pages of Scripture, there is an inextricable link between preaching and sanctification. Behind it all is the simple principle that the Word of God proclaimed produces maturity in the hearts of God's people. If you want to grow in the Lord, you need to submit to faithful preaching as a means of grace.

---

[22] D. Martyn Lloyd-Jones, ed. Kevin DeYoung, *Preaching and Preachers: 40th Anniversary Edition* (Grand Rapids: Zondervan Publishing, 2011), 17.

THE "MEANS OF GRACE"

At this point, it may be helpful to explain the meaning of the term "means of grace." As we saw in the last chapter, God did not leave us on our own to figure out how spiritual growth happens. He revealed the pattern of sanctification in the Bible and provided us with external helps so that we can follow the biblical pattern. These external instruments are the divinely-ordained means by which we encounter God's grace. For example, God graciously promised to care for us as His children, and one of the means He uses to fulfill this promise is prayer (cf. Luke 11:10-13). God is not bound by our prayers, but He has chosen to use them as He pours out His grace upon us. This is how the means of grace, of which there are many, function. They do not force God to act against His will, nor do they earn the benefits of grace. They are simply external instruments assigned and employed by God for our good.

Objective grace

God could have chosen to show us His grace directly without mediation, but we should be very thankful that He has chosen to use objective and identifiable means to dispense His grace. His design makes visible the grace that would otherwise be invisible. He shows us specifically where we can go to feast on the benefits of His favor toward us. This is so helpful, in part because it provides an objective mooring for the subjective experience of the Christian life. Understanding the objective instruments God uses to sanctify you is of paramount importance if you want to "grow in the grace and knowledge of our Lord and Savior Jesus Christ" (2 Pt 3:18). God has not promised to mystically mature you as you recite the gospel to yourself. Instead, God has extended His sanctifying grace to you through specific means. If you're passively waiting to get "zapped" with growth, your soul will shrivel up long before it is ever strengthened. Maturity comes as we actively expose ourselves to the means of grace God has revealed to us. In other words, don't be surprised by a lack of growth when you separate yourself from the means of grace.

As a pastor, I see confusion on this issue all the time. People who sporadically attend church and rarely read their Bibles will come to me befuddled by their struggles with sin. They just can't figure out why they keep falling into sin and why the Christian life seems so hard. What they fail to realize is that they have separated themselves from all the provisions of grace God has promised to use in their lives. As a result, they are seeking victory in the Christian life by their own strength rather than by the grace of God. Additionally, they are walking by sight, not faith. Their Christian life is rooted in what they can see and experience, rather than what God has promised them. It feels so hard to get to church on Sunday morning, so they reject the promise of grace through corporate worship. Immersion in God's Word through preaching and personal study does not provide the immediate relief from temptation they hoped for, so they succumb to gratification for relief. They expect growth apart from grace, detached from truth, and without faith. As we saw in the last chapter, that will never work. What they really need to do is discipline themselves to run toward the means of grace in search of growth.

Diligence in grace

We have been invited to participate in our spiritual growth through the means of grace. God does not need our participation, but He has promised to bless our humble diligence in pursuing His grace. In some corners of evangelicalism it may be viewed as legalistic to counsel a struggling Christian to seek the practical means of grace through personal disciplines. In fact, some of the most popular teaching in the church today would have you pursue almost anything but diligent obedience:

- "Live your life with such freedom that uptight Christians doubt your salvation."[23]

- "[Jesus] is So Much Better Than Trying Harder, Doing More, and Being Good Enough."[24]

- "Jesus + nothing = everything."[25]

These are the mantras of our day, and you can sell a lot of books with slogans likes these. But there is a reason why empty platitudes such as these resonate with such a broad constituency—they appeal to the natural man. In this paradigm the means of growth is passivity, and the result of growth is personal affirmation. What a message! You don't have to put forth any effort for your sanctification, and you don't have to feel bad about it, either. It is an emotional prosperity gospel that promises people the visceral benefits of sanctification without the strenuous effort of maturing. Spiritually, you can have your cake and eat it too; the joy of communion

---

[23] Steve Brown, https://www.keylife.org/articles/living-as-a-free-christian, accessed 10/26/2018.

[24] Jefferson Bethke, Jesus > Religion: Why He Is So Much Better Than Trying Harder, Doing More, and Being Good Enough (Nashville, TN: Thomas Nelson, 2013).

[25] Tullian Tchividjian, Jesus + nothing = everything (Wheaton, IL: Crossway, 2011).

with God without the pain of separation from this world. Of course, the problem with this view is that God did not design us to grow this way.

Passivity for personal affirmation does not strengthen faith, and practicing spiritual disciplines for personal growth does not violate grace. When we cling to the practical means of grace, it is an act of humility before the God who graciously uses these instruments for our sanctification. Remember, the same God who despises legalistic efforts to earn His favor also prescribes faith-filled effort to experience growth. In fact, if we seek to grow apart from the means of grace, we are striving in our own efforts, even if we call it grace.

We can run our race on one of two paths. We can follow the path of self-effort marked out by human machinations, or we can follow the path of grace marked out by the means of grace. We can walk by our feelings or by faith; we can strive in our power or God's power; we can trust our opinions or God's truth; we can seek growth through carnal devices or God's promises. The bottom line is that when we detach ourselves from the disciplines God commanded and promised to bless, we are seeking sanctification on our terms. This, of course, will never work. If we want to grow in grace, we must do so on God's terms, not our own. We must obediently do what God has commanded us to do, and trust God to bless our obedience with spiritual growth. This means that we must utilize the means of grace in the work of sanctification.

PREACHING AS A MEANS OF GRACE

Of all the means of grace God has designed for our growth, none is more powerful than the preached Word. Few would disagree that preaching plays some role in the growth and maturation of a Christian. Even though preaching has fallen on hard times, the vast majority of Christians still affirm some role for preaching in the church. So, if I said that preaching was *a* means of grace for sanctification, with the exception of a few fringe voices, I don't think many Evangelical Christians would disagree with that statement. In fact, if I said that preaching was a really important means of grace for sanctification, there might be fewer people who would agree with me, but I wouldn't be left standing alone. However, I am arguing for more than this. My contention is that preaching is *the* most important means of grace for sanctification. With this assertion, I have traversed past the comfort zone of many, and not-so-subtly violated the praxis of most churches. In creed and practice, Christians today simply do not look to preaching as a way to grow. For too many, preaching may play *a* role in the Christian life, but it is not *the* role God intends.

Let me be quick to add, it is not impossible for a Christian to mature without faithful preaching. God can and does utilize means of grace besides preaching. Personal study, prayer, applying truth to your circumstances, and many other godly disciplines are all legitimate means of growth. If you do not have a solid local church accessible to you, or you are imprisoned for your faith, you can still mature in the Lord by God's grace. Preaching is not the solitary means of grace in the Christian life, however, it is the most ordinary, and impactful means of grace for sanctification.[26]

The proven history of preaching

Think about it from an historical perspective. Preaching has always played a part in the spiritual maturity of the church. This pattern began with Jesus, who only had three years of ministry on this earth to prepare the world for the cross. So what did he do with this precious time? More than anything else, Jesus devoted His ministry to preaching and teaching. According to Mark 1:15, Jesus publicly launched His ministry when he "came into Galilee, proclaiming the gospel of God, and saying, 'The time is fulfilled, and the kingdom of God is at hand; repent and believe in the gospel.'" Jesus, who certainly understood the best method of evangelism and shepherding, employed preaching as His primary tool.

The disciples often struggled to understand the emphasis Jesus placed on preaching. In the beginning their priority was to reach as many people as possible, which did not always fit with Jesus's priority to preach as much as possible. As Mark 1:35-39 demonstrates, this tension appeared very early in Jesus's ministry:

> And rising very early in the morning, while it was still dark, he departed and went out to a desolate place, and there he prayed. And Simon and those who were with him searched for him, and they found him and said to him, "Everyone is looking for you." And he said to them, "Let us go on to the next towns, that I may preach there also, for that is why I came out." And he went throughout all Galilee, preaching in their synagogues and casting out demons.

---

[26] Personal and corporate prayer are vital means of grace as well, but as previously stated, they must be informed by the truth of God's Word—and preaching is historically, practically, and biblically the pre-eminent means by which a disciple receives the Word of God.

Even though it was counterintuitive for the disciples, Jesus oriented His ministry around preaching because he understood the saving and sanctifying power of God's Word. Eventually the apostles understood Jesus's high view of preaching. Acts 6:4 reveals that in Jerusalem the apostles emulated Jesus by devoting themselves to "prayer and to the ministry of the word." Even Paul, the last-born apostle, was sent by Christ to "preach the gospel" (1 Cor 1:17). This is how preaching for salvation and sanctification became the lynchpin for ministry in the NT church, and this commitment was passed on to the next generation of pastors. When Paul commanded Timothy to "preach the word" (2 Tim 4:2) he established the priority of preaching for every pastor thereafter.

The Church Fathers, in the decades after the completion of the New Testament, followed suit by maintaining a commitment to the preeminence of the preached word in the church. As Garvie eloquently asserts, "Probably there had never been in human history a period in which preaching had been so widely and keenly appreciated, as when the Christian Church went forth to conquer the world by 'the foolishness of preaching.'"[27] The greatest preacher of the early church may have been Chrysostom, and he maintained that the "teaching of the Word… is the best instrument"[28] for spiritual growth.

The power of preaching was again demonstrated in the Reformation. Luther wrote his *Ninety-Five Theses*, but it was his preaching that enlivened the spiritual life of his generation. Calvin set the standard for systematic theologies with his *Institutes of the Christian Religion*, but it was his preaching that transformed the city of Geneva. Zwingli's expository series in Matthew was so powerful that city leaders mandated that all preaching in Zurich be expository. The spirit of the Reformation was delivered, nurtured, and matured from the pulpit.

The pattern of church history is growth through preaching. Time and time again, Church history demonstrates the importance of preaching. The Puritan pulpit propelled the burgeoning Reformed church forward, the evangelistic pulpits of the Great Awakening woke up a sleeping church, and the expository resurgence of the contemporary church refocused a distracted church. The doctrinal truth standing behind the role of preaching in the history of the church is that preaching is the primary means of grace. In fact, for nearly two thousand years Christians had to grow through preaching because they didn't have their own copy of the Bible. It is only a

---

[27] A.E. Garvie, *The Christian Preacher* (New York: Charles Scribner's Sons, 1921), 59.
[28] Ibid., 114-115.

recent development that Christians have been able to own and read personal copies of the Scripture in a language they understand. For the majority of Church history preaching has been the primary means of grace for spiritual growth, and I am convinced that it is still true today.

The biblical promise of preaching

Ultimately, the importance of preaching is not determined by church history. Preaching is important because God determined to accomplish His saving and sanctifying purposes through the preaching of the Word. There is power for sanctification in preaching because God designed us to spiritually feed on the preaching of the Word. This is why, in addition to providing the church with His truth, God sends messengers to proclaim His truth. He gave the truth for the purpose of sanctification, and He designed preaching to animate that truth.

One of the most neglected promises of the OT is found in Jeremiah 3:15, where God promised to send "shepherds after my own heart, who will feed you with knowledge and understanding." Ultimately, Jesus fulfills this promise as the Great Shepherd who leads and feeds His people like none before or since. However, Jesus is not the sole fulfillment of this prophecy. In keeping with His promise, Christ also sends under-shepherds to His people—pastors who feed the flock through the ministry of the Word. Through the preaching ministry of promised shepherds, God pours out His grace on His people and propels His kingdom work forward. In other words, faithful preaching from faithful men is a provision of grace from God.

Conversely, the absence of faithful preaching reflects God's judgment on a people. Amos 8:11-12 illustrates this point:

> "Behold, the days are coming," declares the Lord God, "when I will send a famine on the land— not a famine of bread, nor a thirst for water, but of hearing the words of the Lord. They shall wander from sea to sea, and from north to east; they shall run to and fro, to seek the word of the Lord, but they shall not find it."

This kind of famine is not the result of a drought of rain, but a drought of grace. The absence of the preached word is tantamount to the absence of God's grace. Have you ever wondered why it is so hard to find a church that faithfully teaches the Bible? At least part of it is the judgment of God on our culture. When God judges a people, He takes the preached word away from them. There has been a wholesale rejection of God's truth in our culture, and as a result there is a lack of true biblical preaching—it is God's punishment.

Despite this judgement on our culture, God continues to feed His people the grace they need through the preaching of divine truth. Without this provision there would be no growth in the church. The maturity and ministry of the Church rises and falls on the strength of its pulpit. This is the pattern the apostle Paul sets forth in Ephesians chapter four. Beginning in verses 11-12, Paul reminds us that the ministry of faithful preachers is a gift from God: "And he gave the apostles, the prophets, the evangelists, the shepherds and teachers, to equip the saints for the work of ministry, for building up the body of Christ...." Just as He promised in Jeremiah 3:15, God provides the church with gifted men to proclaim His Word. This public ministry of the Word has both an individual and corporate place as individual Christians are equipped, and the entire church is built up through preaching. In other words, the biblical strategy for personal sanctification and church growth is the preaching of the Word.

Some might balk at this strategy of relying on the foolishness of preaching to build the church as impractical and destined to fail. However, Paul explains the results of biblical preaching in verses 13-16:

> ...until we all attain to the unity of the faith and of the knowledge of the Son of God, to mature manhood, to the measure of the stature of the fullness of Christ, so that we may no longer be children, tossed to and fro by the waves and carried about by every wind of doctrine, by human cunning, by craftiness in deceitful schemes. Rather, speaking the truth in love, we are to grow up in every way into him who is the head, into Christ, from whom the whole body, joined and held together by every joint with which it is equipped, when each part is working properly, makes the body grow so that it builds itself up in love."

Had Paul's goal been to gather a crowd, he no doubt would have emphasized innovative strategies for doing so. However, Paul's goal–which should be our goal–was to mature the church. Paul understood that the maturity of the church will never outpace the maturity of the pulpit, because the spiritual growth of the congregation is an outflow of the spiritual power in preaching. For the church to mature, there must be mature preaching from a mature man.

The present need for preaching

Sadly, many churches and movements value marketability rather than maturity in the preacher, but this is not God's design. The church needs pastor-teachers, not celebrity-personalities. "Tweetable" sermons delivered by marketable personalities may bring in big dollars, but they won't produce sanctification. The cult of personality may be drawn to a man who can create and cement a brand for himself, but the church needs faithful men to faithfully proclaim the Word. Healthy preaching produces healthy Christians and "lame sermonettes produce Christianettes."29 The church needs to wake up and recognize this reality. Faithfulness in the church requires faithfulness in preaching. It does not stop there, but it always begins there. This is not just true of the church corporately; it is true of you individually. You need to recognize that your maturity depends on the maturity of the preaching that you listen to. Your growth hinges on whether you are feasting on faithful preaching or floundering in a famine of preaching. *The Church—individually and corporately—is brought into mature manhood through the public proclamation of the Word of God.*

---

[29] R. Kent Hughes, *Ephesians: The Mystery of the Body of Christ,* PTW (Wheaton, IL: Crossway Books, 1990), 134.

6
ESPECIALLY PREACHING

There is no strategy for growth more powerful than preaching. This strategy has been proven through the years. The Reformation swept through a largely illiterate Europe as people heard the Word. In the thousands of years before personal copies of the Bible were available and affordable, God's people fed on the proclamation of the Word. In the Old Testament, God promised shepherds to feed us with faithful preaching, and He kept that promise to the church. Jesus, Peter, Paul, the Church Fathers, and the Reformers all saw revival when the Word was made public. There is no other means of grace more prominent or powerful, and this is by God's design. Preaching is a time-tested, divinely authorized source of sanctifying grace.

There is no question that preaching is a means of grace, but maybe you are still not sure that it is the most important resource for your Christian growth. After all, personal study, regular prayer, and the church ordinances are pretty important. Despite all that has been said thus far, if you are skeptical about the preeminence of preaching in your sanctification, let me try to persuade you with seven reasons why preaching possesses an irreplaceable power for your sanctification. As we work through these reasons, notice how they correlate with the mechanics of sanctification we studied in a previous chapter. God designed the power of preaching to correspond with the process of sanctification.

REASON 1: PREACHING PROVIDES GRACE

We simply cannot progress in the Christian life apart from the benefits of God's kind disposition toward us, and the fresh breeze of God's sanctifying grace blows most consistently in the shadow of the pulpit. Preaching is a sanctifying transaction between God and His people. God graciously meets with us through the preaching of the Word and provides us with an objective means of communing with Him. Not only does God graciously make His presence known to us through preaching, He also confirms His grace for us through preaching. Consider Titus 2:11-14:

> For the grace of God has appeared, bringing salvation for all people, training us to renounce ungodliness and worldly passions, and to live self-controlled, upright, and godly lives in the present age, waiting for our blessed hope, the appearing of the glory of our great God and Savior Jesus Christ, who gave himself for us to redeem us from all lawlessness and to purify for himself a people for his own possession who are zealous for good works.

In this passage we see the fullness of God's grace, which saves us through redemption and trains us in righteousness. What does this have to do with preaching? The context of Titus chapter two is the public teaching ministry of Titus. Paul commanded Titus to "teach what accords with sound doctrine" (v. 1) and "declare these things; exhort and rebuke with all authority…" (v. 15). The saving and sanctifying grace found in verses 11-14 is the cause and the content of preaching.[30] Preaching is sanctifying because God communes with His people and confirms His grace through it.

REASON 2: PREACHING PROCLAIMS TRUTH

Another reason preaching for sanctification is the primary means of spiritual growth is that it proclaims the truth. At this point a disclaimer is necessary: not all preaching proclaims truth; in fact, most preaching does not. Much of what passes for preaching is vanity embodied in twenty-five minutes' worth of words. Vain preaching consists of stories, opinions, and premonitions, which makes it completely subjective and man-centered. This kind of preaching will not produce spiritual growth—in fact, from a biblical perspective this kind of preaching should not be considered preaching.

True biblical preaching sanctifies us by proclaiming and applying truth. It plunges God's people into the depths of sanctifying truth and lifts their

---

[30] Verse 11 begins with an explanatory γὰρ (*gar*), which indicates that this grace is the reason for the ministry to which Titus was exhorted in vv. 1-10. Additionally, in v. 15 the "things" Titus was to proclaim include the grace Paul just explained. Thus, God's saving and sanctifying grace are the cause and content of preaching.

gaze unto the heights of God's revealed glory. Remember, truth is the catalyst of sanctification, and preaching ignites the church with truth. "Preaching and teaching the Word puts it at the forefront of people's minds as no other form of ministry can."[31] Colossians 3:16 commands us to "let the word of Christ dwell richly in you" and shows us that the primary way we obey this command is through "teaching and admonishing one another in all wisdom." The sanctifying truth of Christ permeates the body of Christ primarily through preaching.

REASON 3: PREACHING RELIES ON THE SPIRIT

In addition to proclaiming truth, preaching for sanctification relies on the Spirit of Truth. Apart from the Spirit's work we cannot grow in our sanctification, and preaching is a work of the Spirit. The message preached is inspired by the Spirit, the act of preaching itself is enabled by the Spirit, and the results of preaching are produced by the Spirit. He provides the content, the gift, and the fruit. "Preaching God's word is the central gift of the Spirit given by Christ to the church. By it the church is built up into Christ."[32]

A preaching ministry that is not dependent upon the Holy Spirit is a failed ministry. As Spurgeon recounted, "the lack of distinctly recognizing the power of the Holy Ghost lies at the root of many useless ministries."[33] Faithful preaching is always submissive to the power of the Spirit (cf. Micah 8:9; 1 Corinthians 2:4). Additionally, the same Spirit who empowers the proclamation of the Word also enables the reception of it. The Spirit illuminates the truth so listeners can understand it; He applies the truth so listeners will appropriate it; and He leads listeners so they will live according to truth. Preaching for sanctification is a Spirit-filled transaction between God and His people. The Spirit of God uses the Word of God to sanctify the people of God, and preaching the Word partners with the Spirit in His sanctifying ministry.

---

[31] John MacArthur, *The Master's Plan for the Church* (Chicago: Moody, 1991), 62.

[32] Sinclair Ferguson, *The Holy Spirit* (Downers Grove, IL: InterVarsity Press, 1997), 239.

[33] Charles Spurgeon, *Lectures to My Students* (Peabody, MA: Hendrickson Publishers, 2012), 207.

REASON 4: PREACHING ENCOURAGES SUBMISSION

Preaching for sanctification cultivates a life submitted to truth in a unique way. Personal Bible reading does not require the same level of submission as listening to preaching in the context of the local church. When you read on your own (which I highly encourage), you have the freedom to start and stop whenever you want; you can read whatever text you want; and you can go as deep or stay as shallow as you want. In other words, it is possible to place yourself in a position of authority when you are reading your Bible. When you are listening to someone else preach, however, you are in a place of submission. The service time runs on a schedule that is not centered around you; the text of Scripture is not chosen by you; and how the passage is handled and applied is not determined by you. Additionally, you are surrounded by fellow Christian who will hold you accountable for what you mutually learned from God's Word.

This is hard for many people, which is why so many are discontent with faithful preaching, suspect their pastor of serial pride, and end up leaving churches. But what makes preaching so uncomfortable is what makes it so sanctifying. It is uncomfortable because you have to discipline yourself to submit if you are going to benefit from it, which is exactly the kind of spiritual training your self-willed heart needs. Preaching, when done right, is designed by God to help you resist the temptation to stand over God's Word by forcing you to come under God's Word. Preaching brings the authority of Scripture to bear in your life in a way that you cannot otherwise experience. John Owen put it this way,

> Sometimes in the reading of the Word, God opens a passage that cuts him to the heart, and shakes him as to his present condition. More frequently, in the hearing of the Word preached, His great ordinance for conviction, conversion, and edification, God strikes with the sword of His Word at the heart of cherished lust.[34]

Preaching wields of the Sword to cut your heart in a way that you could never do on your own. You need preaching for sanctification if for no other reason than to make sure that you are submitting to the authority of the Bible and not just puffing yourself up with knowledge about the Bible.

---

[34] John Owen, *The Mortification of Sin*, 62-63.

Consider Paul's charge to Timothy in 2 Timothy 4:1-2:

> I charge you in the presence of God and of Christ Jesus, who is to judge the living and the dead, and by his appearing and his kingdom: preach the word; be ready in season and out of season; reprove, rebuke, and exhort, with complete patience and teaching.

Preaching, with all its reproving, rebuking, and exhorting, requires submission to the Word of God. It is not just the preacher who assists you in this way, the entire church comes together to hear the truth and encourage one another in the truth. When you sit under the preaching of the Word in the context of the local church, you receive the added benefit of an entire body of believers holding you accountable for what you heard together. This does not happen when the only truth you get comes from personal study, individual experience, and online reading. David, who was a man after God's own heart, needed the prophet Nathan to expose his heart. In the same way, you need the Word preached to you to expose your heart. Preaching sanctifies because it places you under the Word of God in the midst of the people of God.

REASON 5: PREACHING FACILITATES UNDERSTANDING

Truth must be understood in order to be sanctifying, and preaching for sanctification facilitates understanding. Some Christians have been reading the Bible their entire lives, but because they don't understand what they have been reading, it has not resulted in maturity. Familiarity with the stories of the Bible or time logged reading the Bible does not automatically produce growth. You must understand what it says, what it means, and how it applies to life.

How can you understand unless someone explains it to you? Just as the Ethiopian eunuch needed Phillip's exposition of Isaiah 53, we need the Bible explained to us. Yes, we have the Spirit to illumine the Bible for us, but we also need the help of preachers gifted by the Spirit. We need someone to teach us how to interpret the Bible, how to fit individual passages into the context of the whole Bible, and how to systematically understand all the truths of Scripture. More than anything else, we need to understand the implications of all this truth for the way we live. God designed preaching to accomplish all of this.

Preaching is not just the proclamation of the Word; it is the explanation of the Word. Again, consider Paul's charge to Timothy from 2 Timothy 4:2.

Timothy's preaching ministry required "complete patience and teaching." True preaching teaches the Bible so that Christians will increasingly understand it over time. In preaching, God uses His chosen instrument to patiently teach His chosen people. Preaching for sanctification facilitates an understanding of the truth through patient explanation.

REASON 6: PREACHING PRODUCES FAITH

Spiritual growth requires growing faith, which is also one of the products of preaching. Romans 10:17 reminds us that "faith comes from hearing, and hearing through the word of Christ." The Bible accurately explained and patiently applied produces the faith we need to grow. The Lord can certainly develop faith in our hearts through other avenues. For instance, James chapter one reminds us that trials can be an effective means to forge faith in our hearts, but even this does not happen apart from truth. Only when we recognize God's truth, especially His promises, in the midst of pain will we increasingly trust in Christ rather than ourselves. Trials are a circumstantial reinforcement of the truth that leads to faith. However, in the midst of trials it is often difficult to focus on truth. This is where preaching is so helpful.

Preaching directs our attention away from our circumstances and focuses it on the eternal truth that transcends temporary pain. Through the public proclamation of the Word, the truth is declared to us even when we are distracted by the world. Preaching draws our attention toward Christ when we are too weak to do it ourselves. Preaching proactively and preemptively develops the faith we need in this life. Some truths we must learn the hard way, but isn't it kind that God does not exclusively use trials to produce faith? Isn't He gracious to sustain and strengthen us while we submissively receive His truth? He has designed us to sit under the regular preaching of the Word so that He can teach us to walk by faith. Preaching sanctifies because it forges faith in our hearts.

REASON 7: PREACHING IS WORSHIP

The motivation and culmination of sanctification is worship, which is what preaching is. Preaching, whether you are listening to the sermon or delivering the sermon, is an act of worship. Sadly, this is a foreign concept for many Christians today, who think of worship as an inward experience rather than an external expression. This is problematic because it removes worship from the realm of objective faith and places it in the realm of subjective feelings. In other words, worship is no longer about the worth I objectively ascribe to God, but the feeling I get when I participate in an event. Hence, many churchgoers consider the song service their only opportunity to worship, and the emotional payoff of a well-orchestrated event as the highest form of worship.

Maybe you've heard this before, "the preaching at that church is great, but the worship doesn't do anything for me." Or, "the preaching is not all that great, but the worship is so powerful that it more than makes up for it." Or, "the worship this morning helped me prepare for the sermon." This is a completely unbiblical way to conceive of corporate worship. From a biblical perspective, the songs and the sermon are both expressions of worship. Psalm 96:2-3 says: "Sing to the Lord, bless his name; tell of his salvation from day to day. Declare his glory among the nations, his marvelous works among all the peoples!" Singing, telling, declaring—they are all expressions of true worship because they objectively ascribe worth to God.

Additionally, how can we worship God if we will not listen to Him? Think of it this way, if you went before a great king to sing for him and make requests of him but would not listen when he spoke, how do you think that would go? Of course it would not go well. So why should we expect something different when we come before the King of Kings for worship? We worship God through preaching by listening and submitting to Him. When we receive God's Word though preaching, we honor God by honoring what He has said. All this to say, preaching is an act of worship that sanctifies.

ESPECIALLY PREACHING

God designed preaching to help you grow. In fact, He designed preaching to be the most important external instrument to help you grow. This may sound new and innovative, but it is actually old and borrowed. In the seventeenth century The Westminster Assembly of Divines made a similar assertion when they collaborated to create the *Westminster Shorter Catechism*. These pastors knew the vital role preaching played in the spiritual maturity of God's people, and they wanted to codify that commitment in the form of a catechism questions. Thus, question eighty-nine of the *Westminster Shorter Catechism* reads:

> Q. 89. How is the Word made effectual to salvation?
> A. The Spirit of God maketh the reading, but especially the preaching, of the Word, an effectual means of convincing and

converting sinners, and of building them up in holiness and comfort, through faith, unto salvation.

Especially the preaching! This is how you should think about preaching in your own life. Yes, God uses multiple means of grace to grow His people, but He *especially* uses the preaching of His word.

If you are trying to figure out where the authors of the catechism developed such a high regard for preaching, we need to look no further than the apostle Paul. Long before the *Westminster Shorter Catechism* was written (and certainly before this book), the apostle Paul recognized the preeminent power of preaching for spiritual strength. In the final words of his epistle to the Romans, Paul concluded with this doxology:

> Now to him who is able to strengthen you according to my gospel and the preaching of Jesus Christ, according to the revelation of the mystery that was kept secret for long ages but has now been disclosed and through the prophetic writings has been made known to all nations, according to the command of the eternal God, to bring about the obedience of faith— to the only wise God be glory forevermore through Jesus Christ! Amen. (Rom 16:25-27)

Paul knew that only God is able to strengthen the soul of a believer, and he also knew that God does this work through the truth of the Gospel and preaching of Christ. Paul's praise reveals that God designed preaching as the primary means of grace to bring about the obedience of faith and strengthen us in faith. Under the inspiration of the Spirit, Paul knew that God strengthens His people through preaching, which is why Paul was absolutely committed to preaching in his own ministry (1 Cor 1:23-25). God glorifies Himself by sanctifying us through the foolishness of preaching.

CONCLUSION

First Peter 2:2 exhorts us, "like newborn infants, long for the pure spiritual milk, that by it you may grow up into salvation...." If we want to grow in our faith, we must rely on the truth of God's word as a new born baby depends upon his mother's milk. And if the Bible is the milk, then preaching is the bottle that dispenses the milk. If you desire growth, then take to the preaching of the Word the way an infant takes to the bottle. Immerse yourself in faithful preaching and you'll foster spiritual growth in your life. Do this by attending a local church that makes faithful preaching the priority. Give yourself completely to that church, humbly sit under the preaching of the Word, and if you are the preacher, wholly give yourself to that ministry. After you have done this, expose yourself to gifted preachers in every other form that you can. Download sermons on your devices, find faithful preachers on the radio, do whatever you can to expose yourself to this means of grace because God designed you to grow as you sit under the preaching of His Word.

7
THE GREATEST PREACHER

No one understood sanctification better or preached for sanctification more effectively than Jesus. Over the course of three years, Jesus relied on preaching as the primary instrument to further His ministry. Additionally, it was the chief instrument He used in the sanctification and preparation of His disciples. At the most crucial moments in His ministry, Jesus was preaching to the crowds and preaching to His disciples. This was the case in Mark 8 as Jesus began making final preparations to head to Jerusalem. He knew this would be His last preaching tour and His last opportunity to prepare His disciples for the cross. His earthly ministry was coming to a close, and the days were drawing near when the disciples would go out into the world as apostles. In this pivotal moment in redemptive history, Jesus prepared His disciples by preaching to them.

The disciples, in Mark 8:27-30, made a profession of faith in Jesus as the Christ:

> And Jesus went on with his disciples to the villages of Caesarea Philippi. And on the way he asked his disciples, "Who do people say that I am?" And they told him, "John the Baptist; and others say, Elijah; and others, one of the prophets." And he asked them, "But who do you say that I am?" Peter answered him, "You are the Christ." And he strictly charged them to tell no one about him.

Peter's answer is the product of divine regeneration, but he still does not grasp the full reality of Jesus's messianic ministry. That is why, in 8:31, Jesus goes on to predict the rejection that will be required for the atonement:

> And he began to teach them that the Son of Man must suffer many things and be rejected by the elders and the chief priests and the scribes and be killed, and after three days rise again.

At this point, Jesus provided His disciples with the essentials of the Gospel by showing them His person (i.e., the Christ) and His work (i.e., death and resurrection). But, as the interaction between Jesus and Peter in 8:32-33 demonstrates, the disciples were struggling with these truths:

> And he said this plainly. And Peter took him aside and began to rebuke him. But turning and seeing his disciples, he rebuked Peter and said, "Get behind me, Satan! For you are not setting your mind on the things of God, but on the things of man."

Peter, and presumably the rest of the disciples, were holding on to a carnal view of the gospel (i.e., the mind set on things of man). Their perspective on the Christian life was based on the sensibilities of the human mind, which could not comprehend the humiliation of the Davidic King. At this point we must stop and admit that the difficulty of the disciples represents the difficulty that we all face. Their eyes had been opened to the truth of Christ, but the remnants of sinful pride in their hearts clouded their vision. They had a new King to follow, but their old allegiances shaped the way they thought about their devotion to this new King. It never dawned on them that following Christ would result in a life of struggle and difficulty. The prospect of their own glory eclipsed their need for a suffering Savior, and the opportunity to share in His suffering.

Much like the disoriented Christians who are struggling with disappointment and discouragement, the original disciples were struggling due to wrong expectations. In 8:34-38 we see how Jesus ministered to these wearied disciples:

> And calling the crowd to him with his disciples, he said to them, "If anyone would come after me, let him deny himself and take up his cross and follow me. For whoever would save his life will lose it, but whoever loses his life for my sake and the gospel's will save it. For what does it profit a man to gain the whole world and forfeit his soul? For what can a man give in return for his soul? For whoever is ashamed of me and of my words in this adulterous and

sinful generation, of him will the Son of Man also be ashamed when he comes in the glory of his Father with the holy angels."

After rebuking Peter in the previous verse, Jesus invited a crowd full of potential followers to join His frazzled disciples so that he could preach to them. He recognized their need for grace, and He identified preaching as the means to give grace to them.

It is important to notice not only that Jesus preached in this crucial moment, but also what He chose to preach on. He certainly did not affirm the disciples' carnal view of Christian comfort. Nor did he rehash the details of the atonement and appeal to His listeners to recall them in order to automatically generate sensations of rest and comfort. He could have done that; He could have pointed them right back to the message He just gave them on His death and resurrection. But He didn't. Instead, with infinite pastoral wisdom and preaching prowess, His message to potential followers and confused disciples was on what they should expect from the Christian life. Specifically, this sermon—of which only the synopsis is recorded—details the sobering realities of the Christian life.

THE REQUIREMENT OF DISCIPLESHIP

The first of these realities is found in verse 34, when Jesus begins by saying, "If anyone would come after me, let him deny himself and take up his cross and follow me." The way Jesus phrases this introduction makes it clear that he had a sympathetic audience of prospective disciples. At this point, many modern-day preachers would have had everyone close their eyes and bow their heads to close the deal, but Jesus didn't do that. From the start, Jesus wanted these potential followers to understand the requirements of discipleship. To be clear, these are not the requirements to earn salvation. Christ satisfied every requirement for salvation through His atoning work, and He is not demanding additional merit from His followers. However, even though the demands of salvation have been met, that does not mean the life of sanctification will not be demanding. Jesus wants anyone who would follow after Him to understand this and to know what to expect from the Christian life, which is why He gives three commands that define the requirements of the Christian life: self-denial, suffering, and submission.

Self-denial

The first defining requirement of the Christian life is self-denial, which is what Jesus meant when he said, "let him deny himself." It is a fundamental principle of the Christian faith that you cannot follow Christ if you are still trying to follow yourself. Self-denial is at the heart of the Christian life, but what does this look like in everyday life?

Self-denial is not asceticism, self-punishment, or self-deprivation. The medieval monks had it all wrong when they tried to literally beat their bodies into submission through external acts of mutilation. The Roman Catholic church continues to misconstrue Jesus' point with the practice of denying yourself something during Lent. The self-denial demanded by Christ transcends physical acts of self-mutilation and periods of self-limitation. Actually denying yourself, in the manner Jesus describes here, is far more radical than denying yourself certain things.

The Greek word translated "deny" in verse 34 signifies a refusal to acknowledge or recognize something or someone. In Mark's gospel, this same word occurs in chapter fourteen, where it describes Peter's refusal to acknowledge Christ (Mk 14:30-31, 72). Thus, Peter's refusal to associate himself with Christ provides a living illustration of what this kind of denial looks like. Additionally, the rest of the NT uses this word for "deny" to convey the opposite meaning of the word "confess." So, if you confess Christ, you acknowledge who He is and what He has done, and if you deny Christ, you reject His person and work. All of this is important because it means that Jesus is calling His followers to deny themselves in the same manner that they formerly denied Him.

Such self-denial certainly involves a rejection of self-righteousness. We must recognize the total inability of our nature and our works to merit salvation. The reality that we must come to grips with is that the righteousness we might think we possess is unable to save, because it is actually unrighteousness in God's sight. If you are coming to Christ, you must accept His righteousness as the sole basis for your justification. He is not a finishing school to put your own righteousness over the top. He is the One who offers an alien righteousness which gives a right standing with God (Phil 3:4–9).

Self-denial also means rejecting any thought of self-protection. Rather than preserving the old life with its old ways, we must put off the old to put on the new. In other words, we must refuse to associate ourselves with the wickedness that not only characterized our former lives, but also enslaved us in enmity toward God. Every description of sin and wickedness in the Bible could be followed by the words "and such were some of you. But you were washed, you were sanctified, you were justified in the name of the Lord Jesus Christ and by the Spirit of our God" (1 Cor 6:11). Christ saved us out of pervasive sinfulness, and He equipped us to deny our former ways (Eph 4:22). We must deny our self-righteousness and our sinful ways to follow Christ.

Additionally, self-denial requires us to reject our self-will. Disciples must live with the realization that we do not determine our path. The lordship of Christ extends to every area of our lives; there is no corner of our existence that does not belong wholly to God. He has bought us, and following Christ means that His will takes priority over our dreams, ambitions, and even desires. In other words, discipleship requires repentance from self-idolatry in order to worship Jesus. We must live with bowed knees and with tongues ready to confess the Lordship of Christ while making no exceptions in yielding our will to His (Romans 13:14).

Self-denial is one of the leading principles of discipleship because, in order to confess Christ, we must deny ourselves. The world offers us self-fulfillment and self-improvement, but Christ preached a message of self-denial—which is what we need to hear.

Suffering

Jesus identified another defining requirement of the Christian life when He commanded that a would-be follower must "take up his cross." For many, the weight of this language has been lost in our familiarity with these words. To really understand what Jesus is talking about, you have to remember that this is the first reference to the cross in Mark's Gospel. The disciples had just heard about the death of Jesus but knew nothing of the cross of Christ. Additionally, those were the days before the cross had become a common symbol of Christianity. The only things Jesus's original listeners associated with the cross was the most brutal and humiliating form of death possible.

When Jesus said to take up your cross, His listeners understood exactly what He meant. He was commanding them to choose suffering over safety and security. Christ requires that His followers be willing to give up their life so that they may live in Him. Disciples must suffer and even die because holding onto Jesus is more valuable than holding on to life itself. This concept of suffering for Christ seems foreign to modern-day Western Christians, but we who have suffered little are in the vast minority of church history.

Suffering to the point of martyrdom began with Stephen, who took up his cross in Acts 7:58–60:

> Then they cast him out of the city and stoned him. And the witnesses laid down their garments at the feet of a young man named Saul. And as they were stoning Stephen, he called out, "Lord Jesus, receive my spirit." And falling to his knees he cried out with a loud voice, "Lord, do not hold this sin against them." And when he had said this, he fell asleep.

The Church's heritage of suffering saints is not limited to the New Testament. For instance, the English-speaking church was built with the blood and bones of persecuted churchmen, two of whom deserve mention here. Rowland Taylor, of whom this world was not worthy, was willing to die to defend the principles of the gospel. His captors attempted to transport him to the stake where he would be burned under the cover of darkness in order to avoid any escape attempt. Taylor's family got wind of the plan and met him on the street in the middle of the night. What ensued wasn't an escape attempt, but evidence of a man who knew what it meant to take up his cross. J.C. Ryle records Taylor's final message to his family:

> Farewell, my dear wife: be of good comfort, for I am quiet in my conscience. God should rise up a father for my children. And then he kissed his daughter, Mary, and said, God bless thee, and make thee His servant, and kissing Elizabeth, he said, God bless thee. I pray you all stand strong and steadfast to Christ and his word, and keep you from idolatry.[35]

Further down the road, Taylor hopped off his horse so that he could walk on foot to the place of his execution. It appeared to his captors that he was dancing his way to the stake. When he was asked about this inexplicable behavior, he simply explained that every step closer to the stake was step closer to his Father's house.

In the same period, Hugh Latimer took his stand for the gospel and carried his cross with him. He was burned at the stake with fellow-pastor Nicholas Ridley. With his dying breath Latimer encouraged his co-laborer, "Be of good comfort, Master Ridley, and play the man; we shall this day light such a candle, by God's grace, in England, as I trust shall never be put out."[36]

---

[35] J. C. Ryle, *Five English Reformers* (London: Banner of Truth Trust, 1960), 78-79.
[36] *Ibid.*, 105.

These men took up their crosses so that the English-speaking world could hear the message of the cross.

The history of the church and the words of Christ confirm that being a Christian is not safe and secure, at least not in this life. When you follow Christ, you are following a Savior who went all the way to the Cross. This may cost you your life, and it will definitely involve suffering. If you got the idea there would be no suffering in the Christian life, you didn't get it from the Bible, which teaches that Jesus suffered as God's servant, and so will you if you follow Christ. This suffering should be expected, but it is not meaningless (1 Pt 4:12-19).

In a culture that idolizes health and security, Jesus calls on us to forsake both in order to follow Him. We do not bear our cross under the compulsion of condemnation like a criminal; we bear our cross in this life knowing that Christ bore the ultimate cross of God's wrath on our behalf so that we will never experience that suffering. We bear our cross knowing that God will care for our souls. This great news is what must be preached to disciples.

Submission

Jesus provides one final defining requirement of discipleship when he commands this group of prospective disciples to "follow me." Unlike the other two, this command is in the present tense, which emphasizes the ongoing nature of this command. This requirement does not merely involve a one-time decision for Christ; it is a commitment to a life of submission to Christ.

Disciples have a standing obligation to obey Jesus. As he reminds us in John 10:27, "My sheep hear my voice, and I know them, and they follow me." The life of a disciple is a life reoriented by the commands of Christ found in the Bible. We follow Jesus by submitting to His Word, not through speculation based on our feelings. This is why, in John 14:15, Jesus said, "if you love me, you will keep my commandments." To be clear, this does not mean that we are saved by our submission. Ephesians 2:8-9 maintains that would be impossible: "For by grace you have been saved through faith. And this is not your own doing; it is the gift of God, not a result of works, so that no one may boast." There is nothing that we can add to the work of Christ that would merit or improve on our salvation. So how can Jesus demand submission of His followers? Submission to Christ is not contrary to faith—it is the fruit of faith (James 1:14-18). Faith that refuses to submit to Christ is useless to save, because it is not genuine.

When Jesus commands us to follow Him, He is simply calling on us to live a life of genuine faith.

Submission does not negate grace. It depends upon grace. Remember, Jesus is preaching a sermon on sanctification, not justification. He explained His work, which wins grace on our behalf, in verse 31. Now He is teaching His disciples about their work, which is only possible through grace. This does not contradict the teaching of Ephesians 2:8-9; it actually follows the exact same progression as that passage which culminates in 2:10: "For we are his workmanship, created in Christ Jesus for good works, which God prepared beforehand, that we should walk in them."

Jesus used a sermon methodology strikingly different from many contemporary models of preaching. He did not encourage people to invite Him into their hearts to be their personal savior and spiritual genie. He did not offer forgiveness for anyone willing to make a profession but unwilling to live according to their profession. And He did not deemphasize the demand of submission on the basis of His finished atonement. Jesus presented Himself as Lord and Savior, and there was no conjured bifurcation in His preaching between law and gospel. "He never held forth the hope of salvation to anyone who refused to submit to His sovereign lordship."[37]

When Jesus preached for sanctification, the demands of discipleship were a significant part of His message. The true power behind Christ's preaching is the fact that He not only obligates His hearers to submit to Him, but He also enables them to follow Him. Jesus perfectly fulfilled every requirement for justification, and He faithfully empowers every believer in the demands of sanctification. Jesus not only preached these truths; these truths shaped the way Jesus preached. They need to shape the kind of preaching we listen to. Christians need to be exhorted from the pulpit to expect the demands of Christ and to rely on the power of Christ. They need to hear preaching on the full power of grace which saves, sustains, and strengthens believers.

---

[37] John MacArthur, *The Gospel According to Jesus* (Grand Rapids, MI: 2008), 143.

8
THE GREATEST MESSAGE

If there was ever an example of the power of preaching in the life of the church, Charles Spurgeon would be it. The great preacher of 19th-century London, is considered by many to be one of the most effective preachers in the history of the church. Spurgeon's connection with preaching began at age sixteen when he was converted under the simple preaching of a lay minister. The simplicity of that converting sermon never left Spurgeon's preaching, which was always accessible to his listeners. In fact, his preaching was so compelling that not long after his conversion, and with no formal training except an expanding library, the teen-aged Spurgeon began preaching regularly. His sermons were blessed by God and a blessing to God's people, which led to a permanent ministry post at New Park Street Church at the unusually young age of 19. From this obscure pulpit Spurgeon's sermons bellowed out for two years until the Lord called him to the famed Metropolitan Tabernacle, where he preached for 38 years.

Week after week, Spurgeon preached to thousands of members in his own church, and to tens of thousands of individuals who read his weekly published sermons. It is estimated that 20,000 people in 20 different languages read Mr. Spurgeon's sermons on a regular basis. The impact of these sermons was enormous and continues to reverberate through their publication in book form. His son expressed the widely-held opinion that his father was a uniquely gifted preacher:

> There was no one who could preach like my father. In inexhaustible variety, witty wisdom, vigorous proclamation, loving entreaty, and

lucid teaching, with a multitude of other qualities, he must, at least in my opinion, ever be regarded as the prince of preachers.[38]

Charles Spurgeon may have been a near-perfect example of the power of preaching as a means of grace for the church. But he wasn't the perfect example. For that we must turn from the prince of preachers to the King of preachers.

While he was on this earth, Jesus established the perfect standard both for sanctification and for preaching for sanctification. Christ's public ministry demonstrates the power of preaching to make and mature disciples, which is what he did while he was on this earth. As the perfect preacher, he carefully blended effective evangelism and exhortative equipping, while powerfully harmonizing conviction with comfort. He never hesitated to freely offer the grace of the gospel to sinners, and he never backed down from authoritatively demanding a response to the truth. So impactful was the preaching ministry of Christ, that faithful preaching is synonymous with preaching like Jesus.

If the church wants to theologically understand and practically realize the powerful role preaching plays in sanctification, then we need to look no further than the preaching of Jesus. This is why, as we saw in the previous chapter, Mark 8:34-38 is one of the most important passage in the New Testament on preaching for sanctification. In this passage Jesus preaches on the implications of the gospel to new converts and potential disciples. This synopsis of Jesus' sermon reveals a lot about what he thought about sanctification and how he went about preaching:

> And calling the crowd to him with his disciples, he said to them, "If anyone would come after me, let him deny himself and take up his cross and follow me. For whoever would save his life will lose it, but whoever loses his life for my sake and the gospel's will save it. For what does it profit a man to gain the whole world and forfeit his soul? For what can a man give in return for his soul? For whoever is ashamed of me and of my words in this adulterous and sinful generation, of him will the Son of Man also be ashamed when he comes in the glory of his Father with the holy angels."

This passage gives us a concrete example of the kind of preaching we need to hear from the pulpit in order to benefit us in sanctification. In these

---

[38] C. H. Spurgeon: *Autobiography*, vol. 2, (Edinburgh: The Banner of Truth Trust, 1973), 278.

verses, Jesus teaches us about the Christian life; He exhibits His commitment to preaching as a primary means of grace; and He exemplifies the kind of preaching that sanctifies.

In the previous chapter we examined the first half of this sermon, in which Jesus explains the requirements of discipleship. In contrast with carnal expectations, following Jesus requires self-denial, not self-fulfillment; suffering, not safety; and submission, not significance. This is what disciples can expect from the Christian life, and this is the kind of exhortation that Christians need in order to deal with real life. The exposition of these demands of discipleship was a means of grace to drive individuals to humble faith and reliance upon Christ. This is the kind of honest, practical, and convicting proclamation of truth that God's people need to hear. That being said, it is not the only kind of preaching that is necessary for sanctification. Jesus did not leave His listeners with merely the requirements of a life of discipleship; He also exposed them to the rewards of discipleship.

THE REWARD OF DISCIPLESHIP

In verses 35-38 Jesus sets forth the rewards of discipleship:

> For whoever would save his life will lose it, but whoever loses his life for my sake and the gospel's will save it. For what does it profit a man to gain the whole world and forfeit his soul? For what can a man give in return for his soul? For whoever is ashamed of me and of my words in this adulterous and sinful generation, of him will the Son of Man also be ashamed when he comes in the glory of his Father with the holy angels.

After confronting the crowds with the realities of life as a disciple, Jesus compelled them to the follow Him with a description of the benefits of life as a disciple. In other words, Jesus explained what it would cost to follow Him; then He described what is gained by following Him. You might even say that He provided His listeners with a cost-benefit analysis of discipleship, and this is what Jesus placed in the benefit column.

Salvation

Above all else, the reward of being Christ's disciple is salvation, which is what Jesus promises in verse 35:

"For whoever would save his life will lose it, but whoever loses his life for my sake and the gospel's will save it."

Salvation is impossible apart from the substitutionary death of Christ on behalf of sinners. This is why Jesus initiated His conversation with the disciples by explaining the necessity of His death:

> And he began to teach them that the Son of Man must suffer many things and be rejected by the elders and the chief priests and the scribes and be killed, and after three days rise again. (Mark 8:31)

The death and resurrection of Christ were necessary ("must") because this is the only way for sinners to be made right with God. To put it simply, the work of Christ is the sole source of salvation. Furthermore, because the perfections of Christ's person and work are of infinite value, there is nothing that we can add to what He has done. He is the treasure hidden in a field (Matt 13:44), the pearl of great value (Matt 13:45-46), a Savior of supreme worth. This is why those who, by faith, recognize this grace and glory will joyfully give away anything, including themselves, to gain Jesus. He is the guarantee of redemption, which is why allegiance to Christ and His gospel is the only path of salvation.

Genuine faith in Christ means that we are willing to lose our lives through self-denial, suffering, and submission—but the cost of such faith pales in comparison with the salvation God promises. The paradox of God's life-giving salvation is that it requires death. Christ's death was required to accomplish salvation for everyone who would ever believe. But more than that, a believer's death to self is required as we follow Christ in living out the salvation that He has accomplished. If you are trying to hold onto your life apart from Christ, you will ultimately lose all life, but if you are willing to forego everything in this life to follow Christ, you will receive everything in the life to come. Or to use the words of the apostle Paul:

> "I have been crucified with Christ. It is no longer I who live, but Christ who lives in me. And the life I now live in the flesh I live by faith in the Son of God, who loved me and gave himself for me." (Gal 2:20)

Jesus doesn't direct us down this paradoxical path to salvation because He is a cosmic killjoy or because He wants us to earn our own salvation. Jesus understands what we usually fail to see, that our carnal existence is futile. More than that, apart from Christ, the life we live, the priorities we establish, the decisions we make, and the desires we pursue will only store up wrath for us before God. The longest and best possible life without salvation is eternally deadly, and to preserve that old sinful way of life only perpetuates death. As Ephesians 2:1 teaches, "you were dead in… trespasses and sins," and that's not worth protecting.

The path of discipleship that requires death to a life of sin promises life in the perfected holiness of Christ. Jesus isn't asking us to produce our own righteousness. We don't have to figure out our own way. We don't have to appease God through our own works. We don't have to be perfect. We simply need to believe in Jesus Christ, the Son of God. And inherent in such belief is the faith to die to ourselves. No one in heaven will look back and say that this was too high a price to pay. No one will say, "I wish I hadn't given up my old life of sin to follow Christ." The glorious reward of salvation won for us by Christ will dissipate any remaining attachment to the things of this world.

Security

Salvation is great, but if you could lose your salvation, you would. Without security there would be no hope in salvation. It would here today and gone tomorrow. Thankfully, as verses 36-37 demonstrate, the salvation Jesus provides for His disciples also comes with the promise of security:

> "For what does it profit a man to gain the whole world and forfeit his soul? For what can a man give in return for his soul?"

Jesus presents his listeners with a remarkable hypothetical here. Think about it—can you imagine gaining the whole world? This is the dream our culture strives after. Every commercial on TV offers a small piece of the world for a small fee, but Jesus is imagining that you had the entire world at your disposal. You could have anything and everything. This, of course, would be impossible, but let's assume with Jesus that it could be true. What would it profit you? What permanent benefit would you accrue for yourself if you had everything? What would you gain if you had absolute power, limitless resources, and unrestricted leisure? Sure, you would have everything, but what about when you die? You could act on every carnal lust you've ever had, but what about your soul?

Gaining the whole world would not profit your soul one bit because there is no security in worldly success, no matter how much of it you have. Remember, the closest individual to gaining the whole world is Satan, the prince of this world, and no one will be envious of him in the age to come. So where can you find security in the age to come? What can you give in

71

return for your soul? These are questions everyone must answer, because we all have a debt of sin for which to account. The most powerful mere man cannot remove our sin (Ps 49:7), and the riches of this world cannot pay the price for our salvation (Job 28:15). The world in all its glory simply cannot afford the soul-securing reward of eternal life. Only Jesus Christ possesses the power to secure our souls eternally, which means to pursue anything other than Christ is to forfeit your soul. Only Christ can offer eternal security, and that's exactly what He does for those who follow Him. Jesus may let you die, but He'll never let you lose your salvation (Jn 6:39). This is why you need to hear preaching that calls you to forsake your worldly pursuits and to find comfort in the security of Christ's salvation.

Splendor

The salvation secured by Christ is leading us toward a glorious end. The life of discipleship described by Jesus may not be glamorous, but the reward will one day be filled with splendor. Notice how Jesus concludes His sermon in verse 38:

> For whoever is ashamed of me and of my words in this adulterous and sinful generation, of him will the Son of Man also be ashamed when he comes in the glory of his Father with the holy angels.

Good preachers always know how to bring a message home, and Jesus is no exception. In this powerful conclusion, Jesus draws our attention beyond the suffering of this life to the splendor He guarantees to those who follow Him.

Suffering as disciples does not earn us a spot in Christ's glory, but it is necessary (Rom 8:17). It is not meritoriously necessary, as if we could earn the righteousness of heaven through our pain, but it is sequentially necessary. In other words, just as our Savior endured suffering on His way to glory, those who follow Him will traverse the same path. For some, this is too high a price to pay. The scorn of the world is too much for some to face and so, rather than submissively following Christ, they shrink back from Him in shame. They prize the esteem of an adulterous and sinful generation over the reproach of Christ (Heb 11:26). They would rather be thought wise by the world than accept the salvation God has bestowed upon fools (1 Cor 1:26-31). What they fail to realize is what Christ warns of in this passage: that rejection begets rejection in God's kingdom.

To put it bluntly, if you reject Jesus in this life, He will reject you in the final judgment. As He warned in Matthew 10:32-33, "So everyone who acknowledges me before men, I also will acknowledge before my Father who is in heaven, but whoever denies me before men, I also will deny before my Father who is in heaven." Whether you believed in Christ or rejected Him will be the ultimate standard in the final judgment (cf. Mt 25:31-46; Jn 3:18, 5:22; Heb 9:27). And if you deny Jesus, you will not only be judged, but you will lose out on the splendor He promises to His followers.

Jesus promises that all who trust in Him will share in His glory when, in His words, "he comes in the glory of his father with the holy angels." The glory that the Father has promised to the Son, the Son now offers to us. When you understand this glory, you'll trade everything for it. This is the same point Jesus conveyed in the parables of Matthew 13:44-46:

> The kingdom of heaven is like treasure hidden in a field, which a man found and covered up. Then in his joy he goes and sells all that he has and buys that field. Again, the kingdom of heaven is like a merchant in search of fine pearls, who, on finding one pearl of great value, went and sold all that he had and bought it.

Jesus is the treasure hidden in a field; He is the pearl of great price. We must loosen our grip on this world and lay hold of Him so that we can receive the reward of salvation's splendor that He has secured for us.

JESUS ON PREACHING FOR SANCTIFICATION

It is a privilege to listen to the kind of preaching exemplified by Jesus. In fact, the prince of preachers himself, Charles Spurgeon, considered hearing the gospel to be one of the greatest privileges in life:

> It is a great privilege to hear the gospel. You may smile and think there is nothing very great in it. The damned in hell know. Oh, what would they give if they could hear the gospel now? If they could come back and entertain but the shadow of a hope that they might escape from the wrath to come? The saved in heaven estimate this privilege at a high rate, for, having obtained salvation through the preaching of this gospel, they can never cease to bless their God for calling them by his word of truth. O that you knew it! On your

dying beds the listening to a gospel sermon will seem another thing than it seems now.[39]

Spurgeon clearly understood how much we need preaching, and so did Jesus. As Jesus was preparing His disciples for the cross, He knew they needed preaching for the path that lay before them. He certainly could have prayed with them, urged them to meditate on key passages of Scripture, or even offered them one-on-one encouragement. In fact, He used all of these means of grace at other points in His ministry. But here, at this poignant moment in redemptive history, when His disciples were struggling with the implications of the gospel for their lives, He preached to them for sanctification. He did not assume that the bare details of the atonement that He had already explained for them would be enough, and so He carefully fleshed out the implications and demands of the gospel for their lives.

Not only did Jesus preach for sanctification, He did so powerfully, and frankly, in a way that is foreign to many pulpits today. Jesus didn't hesitate to preach imperatives: "let him deny himself and take up his cross and follow me." He did not shrink back from appealing to the ongoing obligation believers have to submit to Him. There is no hint of concern from Jesus that a message like this would undermine the free grace of justification. Furthermore, Jesus did not shrink from warning His listeners that if they did not follow Him in faith they would "forfeit their souls" and He would "be ashamed" of them.

But Jesus didn't stop there, He also appealed to His glory to compel His listeners to respond. He pointed to the requirements and the rewards of discipleship. He blended gospel comfort, eternal reward, and ongoing duty in His preaching for sanctification. Jesus's view of sanctification included self-denial, suffering, and submission. He did not soft-peddle the realities of the Christian life as if discipleship would be easy. The grace He preached was a full grace, resulting in the forgiveness of sinners and the faithfulness of saints. He commanded His disciples to follow Him in a life of glorious servitude, and rejected the idea of a life liberated unto carnal pursuits. Jesus did not hesitate to hold these truth before His disciples in order to motivate them in the Christian life, and this is the kind of preaching the church needs today.

---

[39] C. H. Spurgeon, "The True Position of Assurance" (sermon delivered at Metropolitan Tabernacle on October, 2 1864). The publication of this sermon can be accessed online at: https://www.spurgeon.org/resource-library/sermons/the-true-position-of-assurance#flipbook/

9
VERSE-BY-VERSE GROWTH

God designed preaching as a means of grace for your sanctification, but if you've never experienced the power of preaching in your life it may be because you are listening to the wrong sermons. Some preaching is completely "unsanctifying." Actually, on second thought, most of what passes for preaching today is completely "unsanctifying!" It is not surprising that many Christians have a low view of preaching, since most of the preaching they've been exposed to is, well, lousy preaching. It is not as if the act of preaching itself—someone speaking to the congregation on Sunday—inherently sanctifies. You can't just listen to any preaching and expect it to automatically make you mature. Bad preaching will not produce good results; compromised preaching will not produce uncompromising Christians; faithless preaching will not produce faithful Christians. You must sit under the right kind of preaching to experience the sanctifying power of preaching.

I learned this lesson as a young believer. The Lord had given me an insatiable hunger to study the Bible. I started reading on my own, attending Bible studies, and taking the Sunday morning sermon much more seriously. One Sunday, outfitted with a new notebook and pen specially chosen for note-taking, I sat listening to a guest preacher. Forty-five minutes into the sermon I looked at my notes and realized that the only thing I had written down was the date, the speaker's name, and the Scripture passage announced in the bulletin. At that point I knew the sermon would end soon and I had to write something down. Finally, after announcing three conclusions, my prayers were answered when he said that the main point of his entire message was that we need to "Let go and let God."

I could not believe that no one had ever given me this information before, and I eagerly transcribed his words exactly onto my blank page. But as I did, something happened. Before I could finish writing his words, I realized that I had no idea what they meant. I looked back at the speaker to see if he would provide any explanation, but he was now closing in prayer without any additional clarification or biblical information. I left church that day very frustrated that I did not understand what, apparently, was the most important principle for my Christian life. After lunch, I got out my notebook and Bible to see if I could figure out this enigmatic statement on a full stomach. After about fifteen minutes of praying, studying, and thinking, my desperation dissipated when it dawned on me that I could not wrap my mind around "let go and let God" because it did not mean much of anything. It is not in the Bible, it does not teach me who God is, and it definitely does not provide a plausible pattern for Christian living. Sure, it sounds great, but in the midst of a trial can it lead me to faithfulness? Can I fight temptation and pursue Christ with it? Does it help me to treasure Christ above all? No! It is a vague half-truth without biblical moorings. The message I heard that Sunday was not preaching for sanctification.

What kind of preaching is the right kind of preaching for sanctification? In other words, what should you look for in preaching if you want to grow spiritually?

Above all else, preaching for sanctification requires one indispensable ingredient, the Bible. God's Word must be present in order for preaching to have any kind of sanctifying effect, because the Word of God provides the power promised in preaching for sanctification (Jn 17:17). Thus, if you remove the Bible from preaching, you have removed the sanctifying power of preaching. It does not matter how engaging, articulate, or compelling a preacher may be; if he is not preaching the Bible, then he is not preaching for the benefit of your soul. Simply put, preaching for sanctification requires the text of Scripture, which means that if you are looking for preaching that will produce spiritual growth in your life, what you are looking for is expository preaching.

THE METHOD OF EXPOSITORY PREACHING

Maybe you've never heard of expository preaching, or maybe you have been listening to it for decades. In either case, it would be helpful to explore the meaning of expository preaching—either as a refresher or an introduction.

Definition of expository preaching

Here is the definition of expository preaching I like to use:

> *Expository preaching is the method of preaching that proclaims the substance, the significance and the stipulations of a passage of Scripture.*

To put it another way:

> *Expository preaching takes a Spirit-inspired text of Scripture and declares, "Here is what it says, here is what it means, and here is what it requires."*

I did not invent this definition of expository preaching. I actually just borrowed it from 1 Timothy 4:13, where it says, "Until I come, devote yourself to the public reading of Scripture, to exhortation, to teaching. Notice there are three elements Paul required from Timothy in the public ministry of the Word:

- a declaration of what the text says (i.e., "reading"),
- an explanation of what the text means (i.e., "teaching"),
- and the proclamation of what the text requires (i.e., "exhortation").

Together, these elements provide the pattern for expository preaching, and this is what a listener should expect from a sermon. You should walk out of church on Sunday knowing the text of the sermon, the meaning of the text, and the demands of the text on your life. The proclamation and authority of the sermon is based entirely on the content of the passage being exposited, which is what sets expository preaching apart from all other preaching. Anything less than this will do less than feed your soul.

Description of expository preaching

Since expository preaching is the most powerful form of preaching for sanctification, it is vital to consider what it looks like in a local context. In other words, if you are looking for a church where the preaching will be sanctifying, what should you look for? This is a crucial question because Christians need to know what to look for, and preachers need to know what to aim for. So, how can you find a true expositor in a local context? What does expository preaching look like in the life of the local church?

First, expository preaching is usually done in a "verse-by-verse" fashion. The expositor preaches through a book of the Bible from verse one of chapter one all the way through the entire book. This is not the only form of expository preaching, and it does not ensure a sermon is expository, but it is a helpful indicator. A church committed to expository preaching will be more driven by the next text of Scripture than the latest innovation of a clever pastor. Your soul needs to be part of a community of believers progressing through the Bible systematically. You should leave church on Sunday knowing that the sermon called God's people together around God's Word.

Second, expository preaching is text-driven. A true expositor will constantly point his listeners back to the text, and he will spend more time explaining the passage than he will on stories, illustrations, or application. He will not preach a principle or truth without justifying it from the text of Scripture. The best expository sermons bring the text to life; they do not make the preacher larger than life. Expository preaching points you to the Word of God and the God of the Word, rather than the opinions of man and men with opinions.

Third, expository preaching is practical. The expositor will expose principles and implications of a text that pierce to your soul and guide your daily life. A sermon filled with facts and data about a passage, but with no practical import on modern-day listeners is not an expository sermon; it is an exegetical lecture. The pattern of exposition requires exhortation, which means people must know how the sermon impacts their thoughts and actions. You should leave church on Sunday knowing what God expects from your life and the resources that He has provided to help you follow Him.

This is what preaching the text for sanctification looks likes in the life of a church, and for the sake of your spiritual maturity, this is the kind of ministry your soul needs. The fruits of personal holiness bloom in the spring of expository preaching.

THE MANDATE FOR EXPOSITORY PREACHING

Expository preaching is not just the best method to employ in preaching for sanctification—it is the mandated method. The extraordinary task of the preacher is to communicate God's truth, and the only way to do this is to preach the text. Anything less falls short of Scripture's mandate and will not be used by God to communicate with His people. Simply engaging in the act of preaching will not fulfill the church's responsibility to preach and will not be profitable for sanctification. Expository preaching is the mandate for Christian preaching and the only method that promises power for your sanctification. In short, expository preaching is preaching for sanctification.

A biblical mandate

You might be tempted to wonder why there is not an explicit command in the Bible to preach expositionally. That is a good question, and it has been posed to me many times. In response, I always point out that a number of passages do command us to preach the Word. It would be anachronistic thinking to wonder why those commands do not clarify expository preaching over some other method. Consider, for instance, Paul's instruction from 2 Timothy 4:1-6:

> I charge you in the presence of God and of Christ Jesus, who is to judge the living and the dead, and by his appearing and his kingdom: preach the word; be ready in season and out of season; reprove, rebuke, and exhort, with complete patience and teaching. For the time is coming when people will not endure sound teaching, but having itching ears they will accumulate for themselves teachers to suit their own passions, and will turn away from listening to the truth and wander off into myths. As for you, always be sober-minded, endure suffering, do the work of an evangelist, fulfill your ministry.

What does this sound like to you? To me it sounds like Paul is calling for Timothy to avoid innovative, trendy, and popular methods of preaching and just preach "the Word." Paul does not use the term "expositional preaching," but is not that exactly what he is talking about? Expository preaching is simply preaching the message of the Bible from the Bible, which is precisely what Paul commanded. When thought of this way, expository preaching is not only found in the Bible, but it is explicitly commanded in the Bible.

A theological mandate

The precepts of Scripture require a regular diet of expository preaching in the life of a church. Additionally, the doctrine of Scripture demands expository preaching. A robust bibliology and an expository pulpit go hand-in-hand, which is why the Reformation was full of expositors. They were committed to *Sola Scriptura*, the formal principle of the Reformation, and because of this theological commitment they were methodologically committed to expository preaching.

The same correlation exists between expository preaching and the doctrine of inerrancy. "The only logical response to inerrant Scripture… is to preach it expositionally. By expositionally, I mean preaching in such a way that the meaning of the Bible passage is presented entirely and exactly as it was intended by God."[40] If the Bible is inerrant in every word and thought, then every word and thought must be preached.

Similarly, the doctrine of perspicuity demands expository preaching. Ironically, perspicuity means that Christians can understand the Bible on their own. With the help of the Holy Spirit and through proper methods of interpretation, the Bible is a book that can be interpreted. Those who resist expository preaching on the grounds that it will be too difficult for some in the church to understand sound eerily similar to the Roman Catholic opponents of the first English translations of the Bible. They said that the people of the church could not be trusted with the interpretation of the Bible, and those who think that expository preaching is beyond the reach of the average congregant are making the same claim. If God has revealed Himself in the Bible so as to be understood, then the Bible should be preached expositionally so that God will be understood as He intends.

The Bible, and the theology we derive from the Bible, mandates the practice of expository preaching. We have a responsibility to obey that mandate by practicing and supporting expository preaching in the local church. At the same time, we can assume that God knew what He was doing when He mandated this kind of preaching. He knew that our sinful hearts would prefer ear-tickling communication over sanctifying sermons. That is why God commanded that we preach His Word; it is what Christians need even if it is not always what they want.

THE MARKS OF EXPOSITORY PREACHING

When it comes to expository preaching, faithfulness is the mandate for a preacher and submissiveness is the responsibility of the congregation, but the results are up to God. That being said, there are several marks of expository preaching that God's people can count on.

Exposure to truth

First, expository preaching exposes you to the truth for your sanctification. We have already seen how important the truth is in your sanctification, and

---

[40] John MacArthur, Rediscovering Expository Preaching (Dallas: Word Pub, 1992), 23-24.

expository preaching exposes you to more truth than any other kind of preaching. When Jesus prayed for us, He prayed that His Father would sanctify us in the truth of the Word (Jn 17:17). The Father answers that prayer every Sunday in expository pulpits all around the world. Sermons saturated with truth produce Christians growing in holiness, which is why you need to sit under expository preaching.

Help from the Spirit

Second, expository preaching embraces the Spirit's role in your sanctification. When we neglect the Word of God in preaching, we are distancing ourselves from the Spirit of God. If you remove the Bible from preaching, you remove the Spirit of God from preaching. On the other hand, when you preach the word expositionally, you invite the Spirit into the process of preaching for sanctification. If you want the Spirit sanctifying you through the sermon, find expository preaching.

Fulfilling God's purposes

Third, expository preaching ensures God's will for your sanctification. Preaching that relies on God's Word always accomplishes God's will (Isa 55:11): "So shall my word be that goes out from my mouth; it shall not return to me empty, but it shall accomplish that which I purpose, and shall succeed in the thing for which I sent it." This is significant because sanctification is God's will for every Christian (1 Thess 4:3). At the same time, expository preaching helps to ensure that a preacher uses his sermon to build the Kingdom of God rather than his own kingdom. It may "empty the pews" of all those who have "ticklish ears" (cf. 2 Timothy 4:3-4) rather than spiritual ears, but if this does happen, the faithful preacher can be confident that God's kingdom is not crumbling, even if his personal kingdom seems to be.

Renewing the mind

Fourth, expository preaching encourages you to think biblically in your sanctification. If you are not sitting under expositional preaching you are being fed a steady diet of topics not texts. As a result, when you face temptation or trial your soul will be anchored by the topics your pastor has covered rather than specific texts he's taught. You'll know five keys for a healthy marriage, but you won't have a biblical undergirding for how to think about marriage. Topical preaching develops a topical outlook on life, whereas expositional preaching forges a biblical worldview. Additionally, if you're not under expositional preaching, you're getting more theory than theology. Theology comes from the Bible and must be governed by the Bible. Therefore, the best way to develop a soul-stabilizing theology is text by text. You need more than slogans to help you grow. You need Scripture.

Equipping for ministry

Fifth, expository preaching equips you with every message for sanctification. If you are not under expository preaching the sermon you hear each week may or may not equip you for the work of ministry. When pastors consistently choose topics to discuss, they also are choosing for whom the message will be relevant, but when the sermon is based on the truth of a text, it is always relevant for all of God's people. Text-by-text you learn the Bible better, which equips you for whatever providence might provide.

CONCLUSION

Not all preaching produces sanctification. I found that out early in my Christian life, and it has been confirmed for me through the years. There is a lot of bad, misguided, sloppy, and downright silly preaching that will not produce growth in your spiritual life. I have been blessed to sit under some of the best expositors in the world, and it has sanctified me more than any other means of grace in my life, which is one of the reasons I am convinced the church needs expository preaching in order to grow in holiness.

Expository preaching is preaching the text for sanctification. The simplicity of it is what makes it profound. It is as simple as taking the Bible and proclaiming, "Here is what it says, here is what it means, and here is what it requires." It is profound in that it articulates the mind of God by taking the words of God and proclaiming their substance, their significance, and their stipulations. There is no better way to represent the Lord Jesus Christ on this earth than expository preaching, and there is no method of preaching more sanctifying. Your soul needs expository preaching.

10
FAITHFUL HEARING

What you hear from the pulpit plays a major role in your spiritual growth, but so does how you hear it. Each Sunday, preaching functions as a supply drop for Christians in the midst of a battle for spiritual growth. However, this vital resource will have little effect if we will not receive it, which is why preaching for sanctification requires listening for sanctification. Every Christian sitting under the public ministry of the Word week after week, has a responsibility in preaching. Have you ever thought about listening to a sermon this way before? You may have considered the preacher's responsibility before God—either in frustration or admiration—but what about your liability before God? The Holy Spirit has given us ears to hear, and we need to use them.

This might seem like a heavy burden to place on the average Christian who just wants to come to church and be encouraged. Generally, the only expectation placed on the congregation during the sermon is to stay awake. But Jesus expects more from His disciples when they listen to the Word: "Take care then how you hear, for to the one who has, more will be given, and from the one who has not, even what he thinks that he has will be taken away" (Luke 8:18). We must "take care" in how we hear God's word because Jesus commanded it, and He holds us accountable for what we do with what we hear. Literally, Jesus said to watch (βλέπω) how you hear, which is a play on words. You need to keep an eye on your ears, specifically how they hear. Or, to put it another way, you need to be vigilant about your manner and method when you hear God's truth. In this sense, every sermon you hear is a stewardship entrusted to you by God. Sure, some sermons are poor, boring, and even confusing, but if they contain any truth at all, then you are responsible for what you do with that truth.

HOW TO LISTEN FOR SANCTIFICATION[41]

This is a serious matter because rejecting truth always has a hardening effect on our hearts. In fact, if you are sitting under faithful preaching but not benefitting from it, it might be because your heart has been hardened by unfaithful listening. This makes it crucial to know how we should receive God's word. Listening for sanctification actually mirrors the mechanics of sanctification explained in Chapter Four. In that chapter we saw that grace is the source of sanctification, truth drives sanctification, faith receives sanctification, and worship realizes sanctification. These four truths explain the practical mechanics of our spiritual growth and they encompass our responsibility in listening for sanctification. God's grace provides us with the capacity we need to hear, the truth of God's Word is what we need to hear, faith must be our response to what we hear, and worship is the result of faith-filled hearing.

Listen for grace

Grace is the ultimate cause of sanctification, which means that you cannot listen for sanctification apart from the grace of God. Apart from God's enabling grace we "may indeed see but not perceive, and may indeed hear but not understand" (Mark 4:12). First Corinthians 2:14 makes it clear that we cannot hear truth apart from grace: "The natural person does not accept the things of the Spirit of God, for they are folly to him, and he is not able to understand them because they are spiritually discerned." Our only hope is God graciously enabling us to understand spiritual realities, which is exactly what He does for us. Every time we hear the Word, we depend upon grace mediated through the work of the Spirit to give us understanding.

The need for grace in listening for sanctification has very practical implications for how you hear a sermon. Specifically, it should cause you to sit under the public proclamation of the Word with humility. Scripture consistently and resoundingly makes it clear that humility is a requirement for benefiting from God's grace (Prov 3:34; Ps 138:6; Isa 57:15; Isa 66:2; Matt 5:3; 1 Pt 5:5; Ja 4:6). If you want God to oppose your listening for sanctification, permeate your motives and actions with pride. Pride is sinful self-reliance and self-glorification that acts like cotton in your ears when you listen to preaching.

---

[41] For an excellent resource on this subject see Ken Ramey, *Expository Listening* (Woodlands, TX: Kress Biblical Resources, 2010).

Additionally, we will never seek God's grace if we are not humble enough to recognize our need for it. This is true in salvation, for which humility about our sin drives us to faith in the Savior from sin. It is also true in our sanctification, for which we need humility to keep coming back to the means of grace God has provided for our growth and well-being. A humble assessment of self drives one toward God's grace. If you don't have the humility to recognize your need for grace, then the only thing that you can take away from a sermon is what 1 Corinthians 8:1 calls "a knowledge that puffs up."

Listen for truth

In addition to seeking grace through a sermon, listening for sanctification requires you to listen for truth in a sermon. Unless you are a preacher, you might think that you have little say about the amount of truth you hear in a sermon. To a point, you are correct. However, most Christians have options for where they attend church, and thus have a choice in the kind of preaching they hear. I am not advocating a consumer-driven mentality where preferences in the pew drive the content of the pulpit. However, you are ultimately responsible for the kind of preaching that you place yourself under, especially if you live in a place where the truth is available to you.

I am reminded of this often in the course of my weekly ministry responsibilities. As the pastor of a church plant, I speak with a lot of people who are interested in our church. Usually these "lookie-loos" appreciate expository preaching and the doctrines of grace, and so they are excited about our church. Sometimes they visit our church, other times they email me, and occasionally they take me out to lunch. Whatever the circumstances, the conversation usually follows a well-worn path. They are in a demonstrably bad church, which is devoid of the Gospel and unfaithful to the word. Their church does not believe what they believe, and their family is not being fed spiritually. The solution to this seems pretty simple to me: come to our church where the Word is proclaimed and help us be a faithful church. As simple as that seems, the vast majority of "lookie-loos" would prefer to stay in unfaithful churches. They know the truth is not being proclaimed, their children are not being spiritually fed from the pulpit, and they are increasingly far from the church's statement of faith. But they stay. They are bound to an unfaithful church by family connections, youth ministries, musical preferences, and the comfort of familiarity. They would rather be the "informed dissenter" in an unfaithful church than a humble listener in a faithful church. They appreciate the truth, but they are unwilling to take the necessary steps to come into submission under the truth.

I am never quite sure what to say to the stream of "lookie-loos" who love our church from a distance and through a podcast. If they are in a good church, I tell them to stay right where they are and to pray for us from there. But to the ones in a bad church who will not leave despite the unfaithful preaching, I am not sure what to say except that if they remain in a place where the truth is obscured and demurred, they will be responsible for that before the Lord, and that their souls will shrivel from spiritual malnutrition. All this to say, listening for sanctification requires us to find the truth and sit under the truth (Luke 21:8). You have a responsibility to find preaching that exalts and explains God's truth so that you can listen for sanctification.

Listen for faith

Listening for sanctification also requires ears of faith. We cannot depart from this reality and expect to see spiritual growth, although the Galatians tried. They had been saved by hearing the gospel and believing it. However, the influence of false teachers duped them into pursuing spiritual growth through legalistic measures. The Galatians had been bewitched into thinking they could have communion with Christ through a different means than the way they came into union with Christ (Gal 3:1-15). Through faith they were joined with Christ resulting in sanctification, but now they were seeking to commune with Christ through bare human effort devoid of grace and faith. Paul accurately evaluates this as foolishness because without faith our good works are not good, at least not in God's eyes. Our effort only adds to our sanctification when it is the result of faith forged by the truth of God. Faith lays hold of sanctifying grace, just as it did with justifying grace. All of this means that you will only benefit from the truth you hear from the pulpit if you believe it.

Listen for worship

Worship is the culmination of our sanctification—in this age and in the age to come. In the same way, worship is the culmination of preaching. In itself, the act of preaching and listening to the decrees of our King is an act of worship. As God's people we come together primarily to listen. Of course, we have opportunities to make our petitions and sing our praises, but worship of the highest order takes place when we listen to the glorious words of our God. The preaching event—when God's people proclaim and receive His word—is an act of heartfelt devotion. When you listen to a sermon, it is an act of worship, and you need to treat it as such.

Not only is listening for sanctification an act of worship, it leads to an entire life of increasing worship. Worship affects every area of life. Decisions are made on the basis of worship; priorities are set on the basis of worship; and sacrifices are offered to whatever one worships. When you sit under the preaching of the Word, it renews your mind and transforms your life into a life of worship for Christ (cf. Rom 12:1-2). The Spirit makes us worshipers of God as He transforms us with the truth of God. This is the result you can expect when you worshipfully listen for sanctification.

The Word preached must become the Word heard, which then must become the Word believed and worshipfully obeyed. This is the pattern of listening for sanctification. Understanding and striving after this pattern will help you to more effectively appropriate preaching as a means of grace in your life.

PREPARE TO LISTEN FOR SANCTIFICAITON

In addition to following this pattern of hearing the Word, you need to prepare for the sermon. Believe it or not, you are just as responsible to prepare for a sermon as your pastor is. If he is preaching every week in the presence of his Savior, then you are listening every week in the presence of your Savior. That should be a sobering reality for you. It should drive you to faithfully prepare each week for this responsibility.

Study the Word

The best preparation you can do to get ready to listen for sanctification is to be a student of Scripture. When Paul preached to the Bereans, it was clear that they had a desire to study God's word (Acts 17:10-12). After hearing a message from Paul, they would study the Bible for themselves, which cemented the truth in their hearts. We will experience something similar if we will prepare for the sermon by studying our Bibles. Maybe that means you are studying a different area of Scripture, and it helps you to see the connection between your pastor's sermons and your own study. Or maybe you devote time each week to review the sermon passage from last week and study the one for this week in advance. Whatever the specifics, the more you are in the Word on your own, the more the sermon will come alive on Sunday morning.

Pray for the sermon

In addition to personal study, prayer is a prerequisite in preaching for sanctification. This certainly applies to the preacher, who cannot fulfill his task apart from prayer. But it also applies to the listener, who also needs prayer to fulfill his task. As a listener, you have a responsibility to pray in advance of the Sunday sermon. What do you pray for? For starters, the pastor. His faithfulness and effectiveness depend upon the work of the Spirit, which means that he needs your prayers. While you are at it, pray for yourself as well. Pray that God would soften your heart and sharpen your mind through the preaching of the Word. Pray that He would prepare you to be confronted with the truth on Sunday so you would respond submissively. You can keep praying for everyone else who will be there as well, since prayer is indispensable preparation for listening for sanctification. If you have not been growing through preaching, it might be because you are not preparing with prayer.

A clean conscience

A major hindrance to listening for sanctification is impurity. How can you expect Christ to sanctify you in one area of your life, when you are rejecting His lordship in another area of your life? Or, how can you expect the Spirit to illuminate additional truth for you, when you have not appropriated the truth He has already taught you? This is why James 1:21 commands, "Therefore, put away all filthiness and rampant wickedness and receive with meekness the implanted word, which is able to save your souls." You need to make room in your heart for the soul-saving word by extricating soul-shriveling sin. Does this mean that you must be sinless in order to benefit from preaching? No, of course not. But life patterns of sin will prevent you from benefiting from the life-changing power of preaching. If we want to fully benefit from preaching as a means of grace, we must seek purity in preparation for the sermon. This means we must confess sin when we see it and invite God to use the sermon to show us more sin to confess.

Go to bed

In addition to the spiritual preparation that must be made, listening for sanctification requires physical preparation as well. Specifically, to maximize the spiritual benefit of preaching we need to get physical rest. Frankly, sanctification does not occur by osmosis and preaching will not feed your soul if you are asleep. This is why our family adopted the motto I learned from a seminary professor, "Sunday morning begins on Saturday night." We rarely accept an invitation or make plans that would keep us out late on

Saturday night, and we get ready as much as possible before Sunday morning arrives. You will be in a better position to receive God's Word when you have a full night of rest, the disappearing dress shoes every kid owns are located on Saturday night, there is time to grab a cup of coffee before you leave, and you do not have to argue with your spouse about whose fault it is that you are late. Spiritual preparation and physical rest will help you fulfill your responsibility on Sunday morning to hear God's Word.

Show up

Advanced preparation is not the only step toward benefitting from preaching. Listening for sanctification requires that you show up to hear the sermon. Like a starving man standing at a king's banquet table, we need to come to the sermon expecting our King to feed our impoverished souls. And when He does, we need to gobble up every morsel we can. Among other things, this means that you must make church attendance a priority. You can only eat from the King's table if you are at the King's house! Regular church attendance may require a complete overhaul of your family's schedule, but it is worth it. Not to mention, it is commanded in Hebrews 10:24-25: "And let us consider how to stir up one another to love and good works, not neglecting to meet together, as is the habit of some, but encouraging one another, and all the more as you see the Day drawing near." As we await the return of Christ, Sunday should be the pinnacle of the Christian's week. This does not mean that it is a sin to occasionally miss church, but for the sake of your soul, it should be the exception—not the rule. That might strike some as sounding legalistic, but we have no problem saying you need to be at the table for three meals a day if you want to keep your belly full. Well, if you want to keep your soul nourished, you need to be at church on the Lord's Day. Preaching for sanctification is never effective in your life if you are not there to hear it.

Pay attention

More than attendance, listening for sanctification requires your attentiveness. You will not benefit from the sermon if soon after arriving at church, you check out. This is where the vanishing skill of paying attention comes in handy. Faithful hearing takes discipline, and usually this discipline takes time to cultivate. Maybe it is hard for you to pay attention during the whole sermon, or you easily get confused and bored. That does not necessarily mean the preacher is bad, and it definitely does not mean preaching does not work for you. More than likely, it means you need to work at being a better hearer. How do you do that?

Practice helps. The more you listen, the better you get at it; conversely, the more you check out during a sermon, the more habitual that becomes. It is actually a lot like golf. If you go to the driving range and practice a bad swing three times a week then you will have a well-practiced swing full of bad habits. The practice only helps if you are doing it right, and the same is true for listening to sermons. Do it right. Bring your Bible to church, open it during the sermon, bring a pen and some paper to jot down thoughts and questions, and then resolve to focus on the sermon. If you will devote yourself to the discipline of listening to a sermon, then over time you will be able to chew more and more of the solid food your pastor provides for you (Hebrews 5:11-14). Give preaching your attention, and in return you'll receive sanctifying grace.

Respond

The preparation you make for the sermon and the hearing you do during the sermon should culminate in the response that you have to the sermon. Every time you listen to a sermon that contains truth, you become accountable for that truth just as if it had come from God. The preacher—if he is faithful to God's Word—is an emissary from God with a message from God. When you hear that message, it demands that you respond by conforming your thoughts, placing your trust, and basing your actions on God's message. Each Sunday brings you before the mirror of God's Word, and you must not leave unchanged (James 1:22-25). A faithful hearer does not let God's Word go in one ear and out the other; he lets it dwell richly in him, renewing his mind, and penetrating his heart (Col 3:16; Rom 12:2; Heb 4:12). As a result, the faithful hearer acts in accordance to what he has heard. This must describe you if you want preaching to function for your sanctification. You must not be like the man who looked at his disheveled appearance in the mirror and walked away without doing a thing. Preaching for sanctification demands a response, and listening for sanctification submits to this demand by seeking the grace of Christ and submitting to the commands of Christ.

CONCLUSION

We are not the first Christians to consider how we should listen to preaching. We may be isolated among our contemporaries in this regard, but we do have historical companions in this endeavor. The Westminster Shorter Catechism dealt with the issue of listening for sanctification centuries before we were born, and yet it remains remarkably relevant:

Q. 90: How is the word to be read and heard, that it may become effectual to salvation?

A. : That the word may become effectual to salvation, we must attend thereunto with diligence, preparation, and prayer, receive it with faith and love, lay it up in our hearts, and practice it in our lives.

This is faithful hearing in a nutshell. We must attend to the word with diligence, preparation, and prayer while receiving it with faith, love and obedience. This side of heaven there is nothing God uses for sanctification more consistently and more powerfully than faithful preaching joined with obedient hearing.